The Ultimate Blessing: Rediscovering the Power of God's Presence by Jo Anne Lyon offers unforgettable images of God's redemptive presence around the world. Lyon, president of World Hope International, brings new insights into the meaning of "blessing." Based largely on her firsthand experiences around the world, Lyon writes graphically and simply about how to use presence (God's and our own) to bless and be blessed. It is hard to put this book down, but the loving and faithful presence of God lingers once you do.

Mimi Haddad
President, Christians for Biblical Equality

What does it mean to be blessed? For so many of us, this question brings visions of material wealth or personal fame. Yet as Jo Anne Lyon points out in her book, *The Ultimate Blessing,* when we view blessing in this way we often miss the best that God has for our lives. Her poignant stories of how she encountered the blessings of God in the midst of poverty and suffering help all of us to realize that God's greatest blessings come not through holding onto life but through our willingness to lose our lives in service and compassionate care to others. This book is a must read for all who want to find God's greatest blessing for their lives.

Tom & Christine Sine
Mustard Seed Associates

Jo Anne Lyon has placed her finger on the misplaced sense of blessing that afflicts many North Americans. With characteristic candor and warmth, she leads us toward a balanced understanding of the good life. Jo Anne's self-revealing style is a great encouragement to anyone who has wondered, "Where is God when I need him?" This insightful message provides exactly the motivation we need to take our eyes off ourselves and see the world around us.

Rich Cizik
Vice President for Governmental Affairs
National Association of Evangelicals

THE
ULTIMATE
BLESSING

THE ULTIMATE BLESSING

Rediscovering the Power of God's Presence

Jo Anne Lyon

wesleyan
publishing
house

Indianapolis, Indiana

Copyright © 2003 by The Wesleyan Church
Published by Wesleyan Publishing House
Indianapolis, Indiana 46250
Printed in the United States of America

ISBN 0-89827-269-6

Library of Congress Cataloging-in-Publication Data

Lyon, Jo Anne, 1940-
   The ultimate blessing : experiencing God to the fullest / Jo Anne Lyon.
      p.   cm.
   Includes bibliographical references.
   ISBN 0-89827-269-6 (pbk.)
   1. Blessing and cursing. 2. God. 3. Spirituality. I. Title.
   BV4509.5.L96 2003
   231.7—dc22   2003019483

This book is dedicated to my sisters and brothers
in the Developing World, who continue to
teach me about blessing.

CONTENTS

FOREWORD

The Ultimate Blessing is full of wisdom and stories gleaned from a lifetime of dedicated ministry, spiritual growth, and gifted leadership. It merits a wide readership.

Jo Anne Lyon is a highly gifted woman, faithful wife and mother, ministry pioneer, and evangelical leader. She has done it all. She knows from experience both the joy and tedium of living as a faithful pastor's wife. She has lived the delights and struggles of mothering four children; she has also administered a major government anti-poverty program, become an influential evangelical spokesperson, and founded an important new evangelical relief and development agency. *The Ultimate Blessing* mines wisdom from all these experiences.

The wonderful stories of Jo Anne's experiences are scattered througout this work, enlivening, enriching and illustrating the book's wisdom and good sense. More than that, *The Ultimate Blessing* comes from the heart of a woman who loves Jesus Christ above all and has sought over decades of dedicated discipleship to place Him at the center of her life. Listening in on the struggles, spiritual growth, and distilled wisdom of such a person is a special treat.

Ronald J. Sider
President, Evangelicals for Social Action
Professor of Theology, Holistic Ministry,
and Public Policy, Eastern Seminary

ACKNOWLEDGEMENTS

The idea for this book has been in my mind for twenty years, and I am grateful to my editor, Lawrence Wilson, for his encouragement, offered on a hot June day in 2002, to "just do it." I wondered how crazy I might be to undertake this project, given my travel schedule that summer, but I agreed. As a result, this book has been written in some of the most obscure places on earth. Thanks to a laptop computer, I was able to work while sitting in the back of an airplane on endless transoceanic flights, while staying in the basement of an educational center in Vladimir, Russia, (where the 3:00 A.M. summer sunrise was most conducive to writing) or while bouncing along the back roads of Zambia with a vanload of travelers (which produced a number of "earth shattering" thoughts).

I offer sincere thanks to all those who traveled with me to Guatemala, Costa Rica, Russia, South Africa, Zambia,

Mozambique, and Mongolia in the summer of 2002. Many of our discussions about the true meaning of blessing found their way into this manuscript.

I am grateful to Ron Sider, who agreed to contribute a foreword to this book. His writings and friendship have shaped my thinking over the past thirty years, and it is an honor to have his words grace these pages.

The staff members of World Hope International have been encouraging and supportive. Without their skill and commitment, the ministries of World Hope would not be what they are today. The future is bright because of these incredible people.

I am most grateful to the love of my life, my husband, Wayne Lyon, who was courageous enough to obey God's voice twenty-seven years ago at a conference sponsored by Word publishers in Houston, Texas. During that conference, Wayne sensed that he should affirm my gifts and the call on my life. Wayne phoned me that night from Houston saying, "Jo Anne, I am releasing you for ministry." I was then expecting our fourth child and felt that I had plenty of ministries already, so I glibly said, "OK." Little did either of us know what that commitment and release would mean. We are still discovering that together.

Finally, I say thanks to my four incredible children and their spouses, who are my best friends: Joella (Lyon) and Dale Longenecker; Eric and Amy (Gebhardt) Lyon; John Lyon; and Mark Lyon. They continue to provide fresh lenses through which to view the world. And of course, I am grateful to the four who currently refer to me as MeMaw or Grandma: Erika and Lauren Longenecker, and Sydney and Carter Lyon. Their hugs give me fresh energy for each new task.

What Does It Mean to Be Blessed?

In searching for God, many people tend to look for the miraculous and supernatural. Instead we should be attending to the ordinary.
—Philip Yancey

The interior of my soul reflected yet another gray day in western Michigan. It had been three months since we had had a full day of sunshine. My spirit was starved for light.

Each morning, the same dull routine awaited me as I crawled out of bed: making breakfast for four children and my husband, preparing sack lunches for the two in elementary school, and doing the dozens of never-ending chores called housework. As I carried mountains of laundry up and down the basement steps, I carried another burden in my soul—nagging questions about the nature of faith in a world threatened by nuclear war, hunger, racism, and sexism, a world that seemed far-removed from my humdrum life as a pastor's wife.

As my husband and two older children left the house that dreary morning, I paused to look at my two preschoolers.

They were not their usual energetic selves. One had a runny nose, and the other said he was tired and refused to go upstairs and get dressed. After a half-hearted attempt to make him dress himself, we trekked up the stairs together, and I sorted through a dozen pair of socks trying to find a match. Two socks went on his feet, he wiped his nose with a third, and we made our way back downstairs. There I was faced with a kitchen sink, piled high with dirty dishes and a breakfast table covered with half-filled cereal bowls, banana peels, and crumbs from toast that had been hurriedly eaten. I tried to muster the energy to begin cleaning, but it wasn't in me. Brother Lawrence, a seventeenth-century monk, wrote that he found the presence of God in the ordinary tasks of daily life. I couldn't. It seemed that my life was on autopilot and that God must certainly be busy with more important tasks and people than I.

BLESSING AND ACHIEVEMENT

Trying to break the doldrums, I turned on the television. I rarely watched Christian television, with all its glitter, gaudy fashion, and chatter about miracles. But on this morning, the first scene that popped into view was from the program *PTL,* broadcasting on location in Hawaii. The hosts, Jim and Tammy Faye Bakker, stepped into our drab and cluttered family room dressed in designer clothes and standing on the deck of a cruise ship. I was hooked.

Tammy had just released an album of gospel songs, and Jim was promoting it with his usual folksy charm. "Oh, Tammy, you're so wonderful" he cooed. "Just let me touch you." Then he erupted in a litany of Tammy's accomplishments. "You've written books," he beamed, "and recorded albums, and you do several TV shows every week. What makes you so great?"

I'll never forget her response. Standing on the deck of

that ship, perky in her perfect size eight dress, the warm Hawaiian breeze blowing through her blond hair, Tammy Bakker gushed, "Well Jim, I guess I'm just blessed."

It was like being hit with a baseball bat. Standing in the doorway of our family room, one preschooler tugging at my elbow and the other making mud pies on the kitchen floor, it was as if somebody screamed in my subconscious, *Look at you. Your kids are sick, your house is a mess, you have never done anything with your life, you are twenty pounds over-weight, and you live in a place where the sun doesn't shine.* You *are definitely* not *blessed.*

At that moment, my boys began to holler for Sesame Street, and I quickly turned the channel. Then I forced myself back to the kitchen to tackle the chore of doing dishes, but I could not wash away those words, now etched on my spirit—*You are definitely not blessed.*

Blessed.

I reflected on how glibly we use that word. I thought of the many ways I'd heard it used recently. I'd heard it from a neighbor, speaking of an ailing relative. "My mother-in-law is sick, so I'm sending some flowers. I'm sure that will be a blessing to her." *Was that really a blessing,* I wondered, *or salve for a guilty conscience.*

I'd heard it from church folk, talking enthusiastically about their congregation. "The church is growing tremendously. God is really blessing." *Cults are growing rapidly also,* I thought. *Is God blessing them too?*

I'd heard it from friends, speaking of a well-known Christian businessperson. "He runs his company like a dictator—he's extremely ruthless. But he's a great contributor to our church. We're really blessed to have him." *Is there a way to be blessed without abusing power over others,* I wondered.

Then I thought of Jesus' use of the word. "Blessed are those who are persecuted because of righteousness . . ." (Matt. 5: 10). *I wouldn't call that a blessing,* I knew for sure.

I recalled the words of a song that was popular in churches around that time, "I'm blessed, I'm blessed, I'm blessed, I have food, clothing and shelter, I am blessed," and I realized that whenever anything good happened, people tended to say, "I am blessed." Yet when struggles came, the word *blessed* was seldom mentioned. Slowly, a question began to form in my mind. *What does it mean to be blessed?*

Throughout the day, that question gnawed at me. As I wound the cord around the vacuum cleaner, I wondered, "Do people who are hungry ever use the term *blessed?*" As I emptied a load of towels from the drier and began to fold, I thought, "Would a person who had been denied a job because of skin color say, 'That was a blessing'?"

I realized that on most occasions when I'd heard the word *blessed*, the circumstances were overwhelmingly good. As a child, I often heard people at church say that they "got blessed" by the service. In the religious culture of the 1950s, that meant that the person had been overcome with emotion during worship. Being "blessed" may have resulted in weeping, lifting one's hands in praise, shouting aloud to God, or even running the aisles of the church. I must admit that as a child, I liked it when people "got blessed." I found it entertaining, and I knew that the service would not follow its usual routine. There would be no long sermon, and the rest of the time would be taken up with people giving impromptu remarks, or testimonies, about their personal experience with God.

Yet this type of blessing was short-lived and had to do only with emotion. Even as a young person, I wondered if that could be all that there was to being blessed by God.

To be sure, emotional experiences have their place in religious life. Throughout the ages devout people have had experiences of God that were emotional, so emotion must play some part in our faith. I thought immediately of the biblical prophet Elijah (see 1 Kings 18–19). At one time, the land of Israel had experienced a great drought and the people suffered greatly because of it. One day Elijah, prophesying the word of God, declared to King Ahab that the drought would end. Elijah bowed to the ground, put his face between his knees and sent a runner to the top of a mountain to look toward the sea. The runner returned and told Elijah, "I don't see anything. The sky is clear." Seven times, Elijah instructed him to go back and look again. On the seventh time the runner said, "There is a little cloud no bigger than a person's hand rising out of the sea."

Immediately, Elijah told the king to get his chariot ready and get home before the rains came. Soon the sky grew black with clouds and rain poured down from heaven. Elijah was overjoyed because the drought was over. He was so overcome by emotion that he ran faster than the king's chariot and raced back to the palace to tell everyone the good news. Elijah had seen the work of God, and he experienced overwhelming joy. As a child, I would have said that Elijah was blessed—his experience certainly fit the definition of blessing that I had learned.

Yet the day ended quite different for Elijah. When Ahab told his wife, Jezebel, all that God had done through Elijah, the wicked queen became jealous. She feared that the people would begin to follow Elijah's leadership and that she and Ahab would lose their hold on power. She responded by sending a message to Elijah, threatening his life. Elijah knew all too well that she was serious. He fled into the wilderness, taking refuge under a solitary broom tree. Exhausted and alone, he prayed that God would allow him to die.

Is this a description of someone who enjoys God's blessing? What happened to the emotional high? Did God withdraw his blessing? Did it end?

Some Bible scholars believe that Elijah was merely fatigued or under stress from his recent exertion. Others have speculated that he may have suffered from bipolar disorder and was simply depressed at that time. Yet whatever his condition, we see that God was very near to him. In his forlorn state, Elijah fell asleep. After a while, an angel awakened him and told him to eat. There beside him lay a freshly baked cake and jar of clean water.

Clearly, God was with Elijah, even when he felt miserable. Whatever emotion Elijah enjoyed after his great success was short lived, but the presence of God remained with him. Elijah was blessed.

That dreary day in Grand Rapids marked the dawn of a great realization in my mind. I began to see that blessing cannot be reduced to achievement. There must be something more to being blessed than having good times. While success might be a blessing, one might be blessed without enjoying a mountaintop experience; blessing exists in the valley as well. That was my first discovery about the meaning of blessing. Several years later—and half-a-world away—I would make another.

BLESSING AND NEED

During the mid-1980s, famine ravaged the country of Ethiopia. It was not the first that the Ethiopians had endured, nor was it the first famine in the world. Yet because of the power of television, the world's attention was riveted on this impoverished nation. Each night, the British Broadcasting Company broadcast horrifying images of emaciated children with distended bellies, flies crawling over their faces, their lifeless eyes conveying the silent message "Help." While sitting in our comfortable family rooms, we North Americans were confronted by the phenomenon of hunger in a world of plenty.

I had read some statistics on the death toll from hunger, but they meant little to me until the hot summer day in Michigan when I got a call from the director of Project Plant Hope, a hunger relief program sponsored by The Grand Rapids Area Center for Ecumenism. The local ABC television affiliate was filming a documentary that would report on both the famine in Ethiopia and the hidden hunger in Grand Rapids, Michigan. Since I was working as an educational consultant for Project Plant Hope, I was asked to accompany the team to Ethiopia. The prospect of traveling to Africa seemed unimaginable to me. Our church had completed a vacation Bible school program that very day, and after hanging up the phone, I returned to the task of scrubbing the floor of the preschool room. At that moment, I felt something like the biblical prophet Amos, who was tending sheep when God chose him to give a warning message to Israel. I'd had no idea of reporting on an African famine. My days were taken up simply doing the tasks at hand.

As I wiped the crayon marks and cookie crumbs from the tile floor, I thought about the Ethiopian children I'd seen on television. Those images fueled mixed emotions in me, ranging from helplessness to anger to a burning desire to make a difference. I knew that I would accept the invitation. I knew as well that the trip would mark the end of my isolation from the suffering in the world. This would be no sightseeing tour. I would have a moral responsibility to act both there and here upon my return. A month later, I found myself boarding an airplane along with a film crew and journalist, headed for Ethiopia.

The first few feeding camps we observed were just as we had seen on television. There was one added dimension, however: smell. The odor of malnourished people, dirty and diseased, lingered in my nostrils. I retreated from it whenever possible. I found myself volunteering to assist the film crew, often doing the same trivial tasks several times as a way of keeping these starving people at arm's length. Although I traveled halfway around the globe in order to walk among starving people, I continued to use the camera lens to create a separation between them and me. I felt as if I could use it to keep death at arm's length.

Then we entered the feeding camp of Korem. The number of starving people there was truly staggering. There

21

were approximately two hundred thousand hungry refugees, counting those inside the camp and those waiting outside for treatment. Upon entering the camp, our team was nearly immobilized by the mass of humanity. As we were setting up equipment, a nurse from Save the Children United Kingdom grabbed me by the arm and said, "Jo Anne, go with me out to the field." My heart dropped to my stomach. Sitting on that field were thousands of desperate people waiting for help. That was the last place I wanted to go. Every few hours a medical person would go out and select the neediest cases for treatment. Forcing myself not to think, I agreed to go.

As we were walking out of the medical compound, the nurse turned to me and said, "I hate this part of the job. I feel like God having to make choices on who gets care and who doesn't." Before I could respond we were standing on the field. Thousands of people turned and looked at us, yet there was no sound. The silence weighed heavily upon me as thousands of desperate eyes looked pleadingly in our direction. I later learned that the people were conserving every bit of energy they had in order to stay alive. To talk would cost them calories and therefore life.

As we moved into the field, people began to gather around us, hoping for assistance. Yet as I looked at these desperately needy people, I reflected upon my own poverty. One month earlier, I would have said that I had everything, but here, I had nothing to give them. What could I do? How could I help them? I could neither treat their diseases nor provide food.

Soon, I was caught in the crush of desperate people. One anxious father tenderly held his small child out to me and pointing to a gapping hole near the boy's ear. He hoped I would do something to help his son. That only increased my feeling of inadequacy. There I was, both an American—a representative of what has often been described as the most "blessed" nation on earth—and a Christian, and I had nothing to offer these people. I wanted to run back to the shelter of the medical tent, back behind the camera lens.

Amid the eerie silence of that hunger camp, words written long ago by the Apostle Matthew began to echo in my mind: "When Jesus saw the crowd he had great compassion on them for they were helpless, like a sheep without a shepherd"(Matt. 9:36). In that moment, my helplessness merged with that of the hungry crowd. They needed food and medical care; I needed to see the world as Jesus sees it. I began to pray silently, "Lord, let me see these people through your eyes. Let me have the same compassion for them that you have."

I quickly called our translator out to the field and asked him to give a message to the people. "Tell them I am not a doctor," I said, "but that I have come to tell their story to the world. I will tell others about what they are suffering and get help for them."

The response was immediate. Smiles broke instantly across their pained faces. Hands that had known hard labor touched mine; cheeks that had been washed by many tears were pressed against my face. I had given them something that meant more than food. I had come to love them, to care about their suffering. I had touched the hem of the garment of understanding. I had entered into the suffering of another.

For the remainder of my visit to Ethiopia, I forgot all about the film crew and the technical work that had so preoccupied me earlier. I had broken the barrier of fear that comes from helplessness; I no longer needed a lens to hide behind.

Our culture places a great value on efficiency. We want to know all there is to be known, to do what needs to be done, to supply all the answers and solve all the problems—then move on to the next one. To our way of thinking, we are blessed when we have, and we are a blessing when we give.

In Ethiopia, I learned that there is more to being blessed than having or giving material things. Certainly, we must respond to the needs of others by doing what we can. If I had had the ability to do so, I would have fed every hungry person at Korem. I had no food to give. Yet I was blessed, and they were blessed too.

That experience was the second puzzle piece that came into place as I pondered the question "What does it mean to be blessed?" I discovered that the presence of blessing does not mean the absence of need. Those who are in want may be blessed. On that day in Korem, I was.

So far, I had learned what blessing is not, yet I knew that this wonderful word could not be defined only in negative terms. There must be a positive meaning to being blessed. I would discover what it was in a most unlikely place, Washington, D.C.

BLESSING AND RELATIONSHIP

Several years after my trip to Ethiopia, I was privileged to attend a meeting on the "compassionate" side of government in downtown Washington, D.C. To many people, that sounds like an oxymoron; it seems absurd that any government could be compassionate. The discussion, however, focused on ways to use the tremendous power of the state to alleviate human suffering. As I spoke with a number of leaders both in government and in the private sector, a third piece of the blessing puzzle took shape in my mind—compassion.

The word *compassion* usually has a bland or even negative connotation. Compassion is what we have in mind when we say, "I feel so sorry for *those* people." That is an honest response to people in need, yet it implies distance, a sense of separation or even superiority.

In our instant age, compassion has come to mean a quick fix. In an effort to deal with human needs efficiently—and from a distance—we've developed methods of "compassion" that are based on control or dependency. The focus of compassion is usually on the person offering assistance rather than on the person in need. Countless social welfare programs illustrate this principle. In order to receive help, the wounded person sheds his or her dignity and therefore disintegrates internally. The result is chronic dependence. Frustrated by the phenomenon of perpetual need, the helper usually burns out, feeling that his or her time and energy have been wasted

The truth is that such situations are built upon the motive of pity, not compassion. Pity emphasizes the distance between people. No relationship is possible when one person pities another. Compassion, on the other hand, is a commitment between the helper and the needy that is based on a relationship. Compassion requires intimacy. Jesus modeled compassion when he came to live among people, to teach them, heal them, and feed them. Compassion brings people together.

Years earlier, as I stood on the dry, dusty field of an Ethiopian hunger camp, I began to realize the power of compassion. The people there knew I did not have cure for their illness. Yet by standing there with them, I became a source of healing. Telling the world of their plight meant they were not forgotten, isolated, alone. My presence—not just in Ethiopia, but there on the field—was an act of compassion.

Compassion is a two-way street. On the wall of the Lutheran Guesthouse in Managua, Nicaragua, hangs a statement made by one of the first missionaries to visit there in the early 1900s. It reads, "I came to Nicaragua to bring Jesus, and I found he was already here." Compassion is a mutual process. In a compassionate relationship, each party is both a giver and a receiver. Each one is in need, and each has something to give.

On the evening prior to the meeting on compassionate government, I attended a reception to which a number of government officials were invited. Early in the evening, I was chatting with a woman who seemed quite interested in me and my work. It felt good to know that someone was interested in what I was doing. After a few moments, however, I noticed that she was continually looking over my shoulder, toward the entrance. Then it occurred to me what she was doing. She was chatting with me to occupy herself while she watched for someone more important than I to enter the room. My self-esteem dropped as quickly as my anger rose. What I had taken for genuine interest was mere condescension. I had felt blessed by her attention, but she had no interest in me at all.

Jewish philosopher Martin Buber tells of meeting with a student with whom he had not previously met. Buber tells that he listened to the student and made the proper responses, but soon realized that he was not genuinely relating to the student. The philosopher heard the words, but was not making any real connection with the young man. Buber writes, "I omitted to guess the questions which he did not put." He heard the student on a superficial level, but not at the level of the heart—he failed to genuinely hear what was on the boy's mind. The student later committed suicide.[1]

Relationships have great power to bless our lives. Those relationships spring from compassion. Without genuine relationships, we are truly in need. It is interesting that Matthew used the word *compassion* to describe Jesus' response to a needy crowd. About Jesus' life and ministry, Andre Purves writes, "he was present for others in such a way that they were made whole."[2]

As I sat in the afternoon session of the meeting on compassionate government, I reflected over the several years since I had begun to ponder the meaning of blessing. I remembered standing in the doorway of our family room on that cold, gray morning, feeling so terribly in need. Then I recalled standing on the hot, dusty field of the hunger camp in Ethiopia, surrounded by human misery yet feeling so blessed. Finally, the blessing puzzle was resolved in my mind. I realized that to be blessed is not simply to do more or to have more or to be free from pain, hunger, or fear. To be blessed is to be in relationships—first with God, then with others.

God had compassion on me. I enjoy his presence and new life, in spite of my ongoing need for grace. I am blessed.

I am, I believe, also a blessing when I have compassion on others. They are blessed by presence and understanding, and they receive from me, even as they give to me—in spite of their ongoing need.

It would be several more years before I would sort through all the implications of this discovery. I had lessons to learn about compassion, and blessing, and purpose, and giving and receiving. Yet the gloom of that winter day had finally been broken. I had not written a book or recorded an album. My life was still, in most ways, just the same as it had been on that dreary winter day, but one thing had changed.

I was blessed—and I knew it.

TO THINK ABOUT

1. What do you think the word blessed means?

2. Has there ever been a time when you felt that others were blessed but you were not? How did that make you feel about yourself? About others? About God?

3. Do you think that God chooses to bless some people but not others? Why or why not?

CHAPTER ONE

THE BLESSING
OF PRESENCE

*What makes us human is not
our mind but our heart, not our
ability to think but our ability to love.*
—Henri Nouwen

She was a small woman, and very frail. Her son told me that she was one hundred years of age, and I had no doubt of it. Family members had carried her for miles through the rugged bush country of Sierra Leone to the safety of a refugee camp in Kalia, Guinea. She was hunched over and walked only with assistance. Leaning on her son's arm, she approached me slowly as if to speak. Her voice was weak. I leaned down and listened as she whispered hoarsely, "Thank you. Thank you for being here. I thought we had been forgotten."

My journey to Kalia began on January 6, 1999. On that day, armed rebels calling themselves the Revolutionary United Front (RUF), marched into Freetown, the capital city of Sierra Leone. Civil war had raged in that tiny west African nation for eight years but had been mostly confined to rural areas. Freetown was a place of refuge and safety. As a result, the city's population had doubled to more than two million.

The RUF had been infiltrating the city for months, and on January 6, fighting broke out. There was indiscriminate killing, arson, and looting throughout the city. The streets of Freetown literally ran with blood. Since any type of public gathering was dangerous, there were no funerals and many dead bodies were simply dumped into the ocean.

One of the ways in which the rebels marked their territory was by hacking off arms, legs, ears, noses, or even faces of their enemies. They were liberal in their selection of victims, attacking women, children as young as six months and people as old as eighty. Many amputations took place on January 6 in addition to the killings.

Meanwhile, back in the United States, life went on as normal. Most newspapers gave the crisis in Sierra Leone very little coverage. Americans were generally unaware that more than 500,000 refugees from this nation of 5 million had poured across the border into refugee camps in the neighboring country of Guinea.

Shortly after the January 6 invasion, I was summoned to Washington, D.C., for a meeting with Rev. Jesse Jackson on the future of Sierra Leone. Rev. Jackson had been appointed by the then President Clinton as Special Presidential Envoy to Sierra Leone, and he wanted to see how World Hope International and other organizations might help to bring relief to this troubled nation. There was a sense of urgency as I entered the room that day. Rev. Jackson was on the phone with Charles Taylor, then president of Liberia, attempting to broker a peace arrangement. Taylor had supported the RUF in the smuggling of diamonds from Sierra Leone through Liberia. As others gathered around the table from the U.S. Department of State, African Policy Institutes, Amnesty International, and various development agencies, the discussion centered on the failed peace talks held in May 1998 in Lome, Togo. Where do we begin to bring peace to this shattered nation? we wondered.

I thought of a recent conversation I'd had with one of World Hope International's partners in Sierra Leone. A few days after the January 6 invasion, I received a rather cryptic message from Saidu Kanu, our Deputy Country Director in Sierra Leone. Saidu, who is normally quite jovial, spoke in somber tones about the situation.

"Jo Anne, I'm caught here in Freetown," he said gravely, "I had come to Freetown to get funds to buy rice for our brothers and sisters in Guinea when the attack happened." One by one, he ticked off the facts: "We have been trapped in our houses, hiding under the beds and praying. We have had no food for several days because we are afraid to leave the house. The rebels have been using civilians as human shields. The entire East Side has been burned down."

I know people on the east side of Freetown. I inquired about them immediately, but Saidu had no information, even about his family members and closest friend.

We arranged to keep in contact every three days by telephone, but as I hung up, I was sobered by the realization that I could not send rice through a telephone line. Even so, I felt that hope had begun to grow in Saidu's heart as a result of our call. My presence, even via trans-Atlantic telephone line, had made a difference.

Subsequent conversations with Saidu Kanu brought new information. Yes, the church, school, and clinic on the East Side were still standing. Hundreds of people had sought refuge in the church, but the provincial minister for the northern province of Sierra Leone, Y. M. Koroma, had been killed in cold blood that day. He was a former church leader and a mentor to many. Fear began to grip the people, many of whom were fleeing to refugee camps in neighboring Guinea.

As the leaders gathered in Jesse Jackson's office debated the future of Sierra Leone, my own course of action became clear. I would go there. If nothing else, I would offer them my presence.

At World Hope International, we quickly assembled a medical and relief team to visit the two refugee camps where most of our target population was living. Saidu began to arrange the details of our visit in Guinea, including coordinating our efforts with the United Nations High Commissioner for Refugees.

Within a few weeks, our team arrived in Conakry, Guinea, loaded with medicines and other supplies. After a few days in Conakry, we made our way through the countryside in a pickup truck. We were ten in all, five Americans and five Sierra Leoneans.

Because the war was still raging just over the border with Sierra Leone, there were many checkpoints along the roads. Every few miles we had to stop and show our identification. The vehicle we drove was owned by Kamakwie Wesleyan Hospital, and that name was printed on the side. This brought us favor in some places where many local residents had been treated at the hospital. At the last checkpoint, however, the policeman was drunken and surly. We breathed a sigh of relief when he waved us on, since the journey had taken much longer than expected.

It was past curfew when we arrived at Faracariah, where we had arranged to spend the night. As soon as we entered the town, a policeman stopped us and announced, "The comandante wants to see the leader in the dungeon, near the city square."

I knew that meant me.

There have been many times when I have not relished the responsibility of being a leader, and that was one of them. I got out of the truck and began my trek down the uneven dirt steps. The moon was full, giving generous light. I looked up to the sky and whispered, "Lord, you are the only one who knows where we are tonight." Saying that aloud brought calm to my spirit.

I continued down the steps into a room, dimly lit with candles. The room was rectangular, and the commandante sat at the far end behind a makeshift desk, an AK-47 assault rifle slung over his shoulder. Four henchmen stood behind him. I had the sense that status was an issue with this man, so I walked straight to him and handed him my business card. As I reflected on that incident later, it seemed a bit ridiculous to hand a business card to a man holding an assault rifle. My adult children have laughed about it many times. At the time, however, it seemed the best way to identify myself and show that I was in Guinea on legitimate business.

The commandante looked at the card, but of course it was written in English, and he spoke only French so he called for a translator. In the meantime, he ordered that the entire group be brought to the dungeon. The others were brought in, and I identified each person. Gradually, people from the town began to join us, and the room became crowded with warm bodies. The air became so dense at one point that I feared I might die of suffocation rather than a gunshot wound!

The commandante decided that we should all sleep there in the dungeon under guard. I assured him that we had made arrangements in Faracariah and that if they would take us to the places we'd arranged to stay, they could verify our word. The commandante agreed, probably because he knew that the guards had no desire to sit in the dungeon all night keeping an eye on us.

Our troubles weren't over, however. As the police officers joined us in an already overcrowded pickup truck, they noticed Saidu's leadership ability and became convinced that he was a rebel. One of the police officers took him away while the others "accompanied" us to our resting place. We had been concerned about spending the night in the dungeon, now we were terrified for Saidu. We stayed with Brazilian missionaries who offered us food as they listened to our story. One of them made inquiries, and we soon learned that Saidu had been returned to the local hotel, unharmed.

The next morning we were led to the governor of the area. Only then did we learn the reason for our detention and

Saidu's arrest. It seems that the drunken policeman at the last checkpoint had reported that Americans were in the area, smuggling Sierra Leonean rebels. Fortunately, the governor was able to verify our identity and reason for being in the country. We were allowed to continue on our way to the refugee camp.

This camp at Kalia housed about twenty-five thousand people, and we were welcomed there with incredible joy. We presented medicine and supplies to the camp clinic, and our medical team assisted the camp staff in treating the ever-growing number of sick people.

Later, the camp director pointed out the area of the compound where most of the people from the north of Sierra Leone had settled. He said, "I think that is where you will find most of your people." I set out across that primitive, inhospitable place accompanied by Rev. A. F. Kamara, a member of the Sierra Leonean Parliament who was a refugee himself. The dust came up to our ankles as we walked, and I shuddered, thinking of what it would be like in the coming rainy season. As if in denial of his circumstances, Rev. Kamara spoke pleasantly about his experiences as a diplomat in England. I listened intently because his narration gave me a strange relief from the pain and suffering that existed all around us.

As we crossed a dry gully, I thought I heard faint strains of singing. I could just make out the words "What a mighty God we serve, What a mighty God we serve." *I must be hallucinating,* I thought. *The arrest in Faracariah really must have rattled me.* But as we climbed out of the gully and up a small hill I saw a crude church building fashioned out of sticks and brush. The refugees had made this place. There were hundreds inside it and hundreds more outside, singing with gusto, "What a mighty God we serve, What a mighty God we serve, Angels bow before Him, Heaven and earth adore Him, What a mighty God we serve."

As I stood there, looking at this crowd of worshipers, I was not thinking about "what a mighty God we serve." I was thinking more about the absence of God in situations like this. Looking out over the crowd, I recognized medical workers, teachers, school administrators, pastors, church officials, and politicians. *What a waste!* I thought. *These people could bring new life to a broken society, but they're stuck here in this hellhole.*

I didn't have much time for rumination, however. As soon as the song ended, the group's leader, Pastor Sumila, invited me to address the crowd. As I stepped up to the makeshift pulpit he whispered to me, "Give the people a few words of encouragement." I was speechless. What encouragement could I offer these people? It's true that we had some goods to distribute—some clothing, some rice, a few Bibles—but those could only go so far in this desperate situation. What could I say that would be meaningful to these people, surrounded by illness and hunger?

I paused to collect my thoughts, staring down at the pulpit. Lying there were a tattered Bible, a wear-worn hymnal, and a well-thumbed copy of the book *Love in a Fearful Land* by Henri Nouwen. I thought about Saidu, and his first urgent phone call to me in the United States. I remembered sitting in Jesse Jackson's office and realizing that I had to make this journey. I thought of the long trip, ten people and a load of supplies crammed into a pickup truck, traveling many miles over rough roads; I thought of our detention in the dungeon.

In that moment, I realized that my presence in this place was the only real gift I could bring—and it was the only gift that they wanted. They had called for me to come, and I had come. No other encouragement was needed; presence was what they craved. I looked up at their expectant faces, and said the most heartfelt words I have ever spoken.

"It's good to be with you."

35

BLESSING AS PRESENCE

Presence is a form of blessing. We are blessed when we have God's presence—I felt that blessing as I called out to God on the way to see the commandante at Faracariah. And we are blessed when others choose to be present with us. Saidu felt that in our trans-Atlantic phone call, and the elderly woman at Kalia put that blessing into words when she said, "Thank you for being here." Our culture tends to see good, and therefore blessing, in terms of wealth or success. We are blessed when we have more or do more. That view of blessing is not wrong so much as inadequate. Inanimate things—and money is the most dead of all things—can never truly bless us. We are blessed by one another; we are blessed by presence.

DEBORAH AS AN EXAMPLE OF PRESENCE

The relationship between Deborah and Barak in the book of Judges illustrates the blessing of presence (see Judges, chapter 4). Deborah was a judge in Israel. She held court under a beautiful palm tree, where people would stream to her seeking justice. Deborah was a faithful judge, but her country lived under the cruel oppression of Jabin, a Caananite king, and his general, Sisera. We might imagine her frustration in attempting to bring justice to a land that has suffered great wrongs. It was perhaps similar to trying to extend civil rights to people of color during the 1940s. The work of one individual meant little when the societal systems perpetuated injustice. So it must have been for Deborah and the people of Israel.

God has always cared for the oppressed, and when the people of Israel called out to him, he answered. I think God must have looked at Deborah and said, "This is a person after my own heart. She will bring true justice and peace to this land." So God revealed to Deborah a plan for the liberation of Israel. To carry out the plan, Deborah called for a leader named Barak and briefed him on the details. Deborah would lure Sisera away from the city to the Kishon river, where Barak would be waiting in ambush with ten thousand men. Barak listened to the plan and realized that it was from God, but he felt sure that he did not want to do it alone. He wanted the blessing of presence. He answered Deborah, "If you will go with me, I will go; but if you will not go with me I will not go" (Judg. 4:8).

Deborah heard in Barak's response something more than that. She realized that he intended to claim the credit for this plan. She said, "I will surely go with you; nevertheless, the road on which you are going will not lead to your glory, for the Lord will sell Sisera into the hand of a woman" (Judg. 4:9 NRSV).

Deborah did go with Barak, and, just as she had predicted, the battle was won. The oppression of Jabin was thrown off, and Israel enjoyed peace and justice for some forty years. Also, just as Deborah had said, Sisera was captured and killed by a woman, Jael. Barak did not get the credit for subduing the enemy general.

PRESENCE VERSUS PRESENTS

Blessing is often confused with fame. People who achieve great things are seen as leading a charmed life—they're blessed. That thought prompts the rest of us to seek personal gain as a way of making our lives better. I wonder how different our world would be if we sought the presence of God as much as we seek fame and fortune. I wonder, too, what change might be made in our relationships and in our work if we sought God as diligently as we seek the good things he provides.

Like most people, I have a list of things in mind that I'd like—a nice home, good health, success in my work. I often pray, asking God to provide them. Since God invites us to make our requests known to him, that practice is not at all wrong. Yet like Barak, I sometimes need to be reminded to that "it's not about me." When I seek God's presence—instead of his *presents*—I find greater contentment and peace. The result is that I usually live and work in greater fellowship with God and greater harmony with others: I am blessed.

It seems that Deborah entered the conflict with the assurance of God's presence. Psalm 68 offers more insight on that battle.

> O God, when you went out before your people, when you marched through the wilderness . . . the earth quaked, the heavens poured down rain at the presence of God, the God of Sinai, at the presence of God, the God of Israel (Ps. 68:7).

The next two verses show the result of God's presence.

> Rain in abundance, O God, you showered abroad; you restored your heritage when it languished; your flock found a dwelling in it; in your goodness, O God, you provided for the need (Ps. 68:9–10).

After that, Deborah ruled the land as a judge for forty years; it was a time of peace. When we seek God's presence first, his good gifts are never far behind.

PRESENCE AND LEADERSHIP

The Bible doesn't say much about Deborah's leadership style, but my guess is that her work as a judge was conducted in the same relational style with which she dealt with Barak. When Barak wanted the blessing of presence (I won't go unless you go with me), Deborah went. She said, in effect, "I won't make you go alone. I'll be with you." I have no doubt that the remaining forty years of her leadership were conducted with the same concern for the relational needs of her people.

Presence is the strongest form of leadership. Even today, when a nation is at war or some other crisis, its citizens feel assured when they see their leader on television. When leaders are absent, the population becomes anxious. Business leaders know that they need to get out of the office occasionally and be among their employees. They refer to it as "management by walking around." I would call it the blessing of presence.

In the same way, the presence of God brings peace in the midst of a crisis. We're blessed when we sense his presence, regardless of the circumstances. What else could account for songs of praise in a refugee camp?

What effect, then, might our presence have on those around us? How might we bless them by simply being there, instead of—or in addition to—the things we do.

PRESENCE AND TOUCH

Mother Teresa was invited to speak at the first Global Forum of Spiritual and Parliamentary Leaders on Human Survival held at Oxford University in April 1988. A hundred political, spiritual, and scientific leaders were invited to speak, and their remarks were varied. The Dalai Lama brought concerns about what human beings are doing to planet earth. Astronomer Carl Sagan spoke of the urgency of using resources now spent on weapons of death to find alternative technologies to sustain life in the Third World. Mother Teresa's focus, however, was on the human person, a being created in the image of God. She made her point by describing what she had seen on the night before while visiting the homeless in London's "Cardboard City."

"They were inside cardboard boxes like little coffins," she said. "There was one man lying there, protecting himself from the cold, with no hope and no home. I shook his hand. He said, 'It is a long time since I felt the warmth of a human hand.'"[1]

That simple remark led to a face-to-face meeting with the Prime Minister of England to address the needs of the homeless. Human touch is a valuable, indeed necessary, thing.

I admit that I don't usually place a high value on touch. I'm not a "touchy feely" person, and when I see homeless people, I generally want to put something in their hand besides my own. They need food, shelter, and clothing. What good is a handshake? But touch is worth something. My friends at the Kalia refugee camp knew that. Mother Teresa knew it too.

I wonder if we don't face this same question of value when thinking of the blessing of God's presence. We want to receive something tangible from God. Yet he sent his son, a person. We experience God's presence through his Spirit and through the sacrament of communion. He has offered to touch our lives. Is that enough?

I spoke at a recent conference along with a man who worked for a large university. The topic was prayer, and this man told of a time when the university had accumulated an enormous debt. The school's leaders had tried everything to raise funds and finally resorted to a forty-day fast, during which they would pray about the problem. At the end of the forty days, they all were gaunt but had no results. The school faced financial ruin.

A short time later, the university president decided to fast again, alone this time. During the fast, God spoke to him. "You're after the wrong thing," God told him. "Don't seek the funds, seek me." As he began to seek the presence of God, the school's other needs were met through added personnel, money, and vision.

PRESENCE AND ABSENCE

In order to receive God's presence, we need to do a certain amount of emptying. Our lives are so full—mostly of ourselves—that there's little room for God. It's little wonder, then, that we usually cry out for God's presence from our lowest point. It is when we feel the most empty, the most alone, that we are apt to feel the presence of God.

Psalm 22:1–5 gives voice to that experience. This is the same psalm that Jesus evoked from the cross. Notice how these words reflect both the absence of God and his presence.

My God, my God, why have you forsaken me? Why are you so far from saving me, so far from the words of my groaning? O my God, I cry out by day, but you do not answer by night, and am not silent. Yet, you are enthroned as the Holy One; you are the praise of Israel. In you our fathers put their trust they trusted and you delivered them. They cried to you and were saved; in you they trusted and were not disappointed (NIV).

Henri Nouwen observes that "when Jesus spoke these words on the cross, total aloneness and full acceptance touched each other. In that moment of complete emptiness all was fulfilled. When God's absence was most loudly expressed, God's presence was most profoundly revealed."[2]

At this point—the intersection of absence and presence—is where we encounter hope. I saw this absence/presence paradox clothed in hope that day in the Kalia refugee camp. I found it interesting that Nouwen's book *Love in a Fearful Land*, which was lying on the makeshift pulpit along with his Bible and hymnal, had these very thoughts written in them. Pastor Sumila later told me that these three books had sustained him and the congregation as he preached and lived these truths in a truly fearful place.

Nouwen also writes, "Praying is letting one's own heart become the place where the tears of God and the tears of God's children can merge and become tears of hope."[3] I saw that truth demonstrated by the believers in that camp. If we do not experience the blessing of God's presence, it may be that we have yet to visit that place where God is most absent and there to find his presence the most dear.

PRESENCE IN PERSON

Every day we have opportunities to give and receive the blessing of presence. We miss most of them, because we have given the duty of being present over to professionals—pastors, chaplains, teachers, and counselors. Yet when we fail to be present, we lose more than we gain in time and convenience. We lose the blessing of being present.

Following the birth of my third child, I shared the recovery room with a woman whose family had come from Italy. We had given birth at about the same time, and about an hour later, our room was filled with about thirty of her relatives—parents, aunts, uncles, and cousins. They were singing, talking all at the same time, and rejoicing over the birth of another child into their family. They stayed until about 4:00 A.M.

Although I was tired, I enjoyed their celebration. More than that, I felt a certain sense of loneliness because my own culture does not value this type of presence. Ultimately, the hospital did not value it either, and the staff finally asked this boisterous, happy group to leave. Once again, professional caregiving superceded genuine presence.

How sad.

There are many deterrents to giving the gift of presence. We live busy lives. We each are occupied with our own responsibilities. And when someone is involved in a crisis, we are paralyzed by the fear of saying the wrong thing. Generally, that is because we misunderstand the meaning of blessing and believe that God must be absent during a crisis. Words of hope sound shallow to us, so we simply stay away.

I'm reminded of the women who stood at the foot of the cross as Jesus was crucified. Certainly they must have been confused about what was taking place, but they would not allow Jesus to die alone. Their presence on that dreadful day continues to affect us, centuries later. They model for us the power of presence.

Most people who experience tragedy do not remember the words that are said to them at the time. What they do remember is who was there and who was not. It is not easy to give the gift of presence. There are opportunities for misunderstanding. I have been absent on some occasions when I should not have been. *I'm not needed*, I thought.

They'll never miss me. Too often, I have discovered that "later" is not the time for healing. Fifteen minutes of presence given now may be worth many hours offered later.

When presence is not given, both the giver and receiver lose something. Simple acts of presence such as a phone call, a brief hospital visit, a lingering hello, a warm touch on the arm, or a shared cup of coffee—yes, these are a blessing.

GIVING AND RECEIVING THE BLESSING

Following our trip into the refugee camps in Guinea, we returned to Conakry and there boarded a United Nations helicopter flight to Freetown, Sierra Leone. The devastation was far worse than I'd imagined. It had been three months since the January 6 invasion, and the east side of the city still smelled of smoke. Charred buildings and vacant lots had replaced the beautiful buildings that had once proudly lined the streets. There was so much demolition that it was difficult to find our way around; familiar landmarks had all been destroyed. It was pure joy, however, to see so many old friends alive and attempting to bring a semblance of order out of those chaotic days.

Our medical team reopened a clinic and stocked it with some supplies, which invigorated the clinic staff. There were various meetings regarding food distribution, connecting lost family members, housing displaced children, and many other problems arising from the war. The days were busy, but productive—until I became ill.

One morning, I awoke at 3:00 A.M. violently ill, my body trying desperately to purge itself. My abdominal pain increased rapidly, and I called for Kim, who was sleeping in the room across from mine. Kim Kargbo is a wonderful Christian and hearty pioneer who grew up in Sierra Leone with missionary parents, but it was her skill as a physician's assistant that I needed at that hour. She graciously came to my rescue. The pain and vomiting continued to increase, and Kim decided to wake John Bray-Morris, a doctor on our medical team. John prescribed fluids, so Kim helped me gulp down some Sprite before going back to bed. As I lay in bed that night, thousands of miles from home, a visitor to a violent and fearful land, and terribly ill, I felt completely alone.

At about 8:00 A.M., I had begun to feel better and was just dozing off to sleep when there was a knock at my door. Kim poked her head through the doorway and said apologetically, "Jo Anne, there are some people here to see you. They heard that you are ill and they wanted to be with you."

I moaned. *Visitors? Now? Do they know what I look like after vomiting for half the night?*

Kim sensed my hesitation and added, "It's a custom here in Sierra Leone for people to be with you when you are sick. I realize that is the last thing we want in the States, but here presence is seen as healing."

I knew I had little choice but to accept the visit. Besides, hadn't I just felt so alone? "OK," I said, pulling the covers up over myself. "Let them come."

A band of smiling Sierra Leoneans entered the tiny room. In a moment, my bed was surrounded by smiling faces, looking down at me. I will never forget the healing presence that entered the room along with those loving friends. They first expressed their sorrow about my illness, then offered a prayer. Some of them lingered the rest of the morning. By noon, I was out of bed, had showered, and was on my way to a meeting. I had begun that trip by bringing the blessing of presence to a far-off group of refugees. It ended with some of those same suffering people offering their presence to me. The gift of presence is a double blessing. It blesses both the receiver and the giver. God has given us himself, and we are blessed when we give ourselves to others.

TO THINK ABOUT

1. Tell about a time when someone's presence in your life was a blessing?

2. When does God seem the most present to you? When does he seem the most absent?

3. Is your style of leadership (or dealing with others) characterized more by presence (like Deborah) or by seeking personal gain (like Barak)? In what ways might you shift that balance?

4. What circumstances in your life now hinder you from offering the blessing of your presence to others? What might you do to change that?

CHAPTER TWO

THE BLESSING
OF POWER

*Joseph was protected from the danger
(of corruption) by his knowledge that he
never really owned the power he wielded.
He saw it for what it was—authority
loaned to him for a time.*
—Cheryl Forbes

W hen I was five years old, the highlight of my visit to
my grandparents was shopping with my mother and
grandmother on Saturday. We always visited Innes department
store in downtown Wichita, Kansas, which had the most fascinating elevators. In those days, elevators were not self-operated
as they are today. Each elevator had its own operator, a smartly
dressed store employee, who wore an impressive military-style
uniform with clean white gloves. These larger-than-life figures
carried themselves with great dignity and somberly asked,
"Which floor please?" of everyone who stepped aboard.

The elevator operator did more than press a button. The
movement of the elevator was controlled by a lever, and the
operator had to make the car stop exactly at the floor level.
Each elevator had two doors. The inside door was an accor-
dion-like grate made of brass. After stopping the elevator,

the operator would extend an elegantly gloved hand and retract the brass doors. Then he or she would swing wide the outer doors, two large glass panels, which opened onto the sales floor. As the doors opened, the scent of the wood flooded our nostrils. The entire experience seemed exotic and intriguing. I knew for sure that when I grew up, I would become an elevator operator.

In time, I became intrigued by another profession—politics. I had heard of my great aunt Nettie Morris, who had been the first female legislator in the state of Kansas. She was the family hero. People spoke of her with admiration, and I observed the great respect given her by my uncles, tough men who worked as roustabouts on the oil fields. I listened in awe as family members recounted the noble things she had done for southeastern Kansas through political power. I first met her during her retirement years. Age had not diminished the vibrancy of her life. Hearing her exploits helped me form a second choice for my future vocation—United States senator. My young mind saw no disparity between those professions. Both were highly respected, dignified occupations, it seemed, and both did something important. I had much to learn about the ways in which we measure prestige and power.

Yet those youthful dreams did have something in common. Both involved serving people, helping them arrive at a better place with dignity and respect. And both included an element of personal power. The elevator operator had complete control over the car and the people riding in it; my aunt enjoyed great political power and the respect that went with it.

As a board-certified, licensed professional counselor, I've learned that one's earliest aspirations are clues to the blessing, or calling, of God upon a person's life. We dream of what we will become. Many people dream of power in one form or another, just as I did. That is no surprise, for power is a form of blessing. God has given us power over ourselves and over the world. Yet with that blessing come many dangers, for of all God's good gifts, power is the most easily abused.

GOD'S GIFT OF POWER

Our newspapers are filled with stories of people who have been given power and been corrupted by it. From television evangelists to corporate CEOs to presidents, people in all walks of life have found that power is dangerously easy to abuse. And the abuse of power—whether in a nuclear family or a nation-state—victimizes innocent people.

The familiar saying holds that power corrupts, and absolute power corrupts absolutely. That aphorism was tragically illustrated by the Khmer Rough in Cambodia. It is estimated that more than two million people were executed under the leadership of the ruthless dictator Pol Pot during the 1970s and '80s. In July 1996, I toured Touel Sleng prison in Phnom Penh, a former high school that was used as the torture chamber of the Khmer Rouge. Dried blood remained on the floor of these cells where people were made to die slowly. One of the women who accompanied us on that day shared her own story.

"All my family was killed by Pol Pot's men," she said, "but I was able to escape. Then I heard that my baby cousin had been brought to this place. I ran to the gate and screamed, 'Where is my baby cousin? She hasn't done anything to you!' The guard looked at me and laughed like a crazy man. He said, 'We bayoneted that baby yesterday.'" This young woman's own escape was a miracle in itself.

Auschwitz. Cambodia. Bosnia. Ethiopia. Iraq. In the past century alone, we have seen too many examples of the corruption of power and the great suffering it brings. We might conclude that power itself is a wicked thing. Yet the Bible tells us that God created power and that he delighted himself by entrusting it to human beings. Power is a good thing. It is a blessing from God.

In fact, the first time the Bible uses the word *bless* is in connection with power. That is found in Genesis, chapter 1, the first account of creation. There we read that "God *blessed* them, saying, 'Be fruitful and multiply and fill the waters in the seas, and let birds multiply on the earth'" (Gen. 1:22 NRSV, emphasis added).

A few verses later, the specifics of that blessing are spelled out.

> So God created humankind in his image, in the image of God he created them; male and female he created them. God *blessed* them, and God said to them, "Be fruitful and multiply, and fill the earth and subdue it; and have dominion over the fish of the sea and over the birds of the air and over every living thing that moves upon the earth (Gen. 1:27–28 NRSV, emphasis added).

God's blessing did not amount to a pat on the head for Adam and Eve. Through this blessing, God unleashed in human beings a part of his own creative power. He gave them the power to multiply and to rule over the earth. It's important to note that human beings share God's creative power; they don't own it. It's interesting, also, that the blessing of procreation was pronounced upon animals as well as human beings (see verse 22). I have often wondered in what manner God communicated with the animals. Since these events took place before the fall of humankind, one's imagination can soar at the possibilities.

For human beings, there was a second aspect to the blessing—dominion. We were given the power and the responsibility to manage God's creation. It's obvious from these verses that we could not do what God intended without his blessing. He gave us that blessing when he shared his creative power with us.

In addition to power, God gave Adam and Eve a model

for its exercise. In creating the world, God was joyful, careful, orderly, and loving. He brought order to his creation, transforming the formless, void earth into a beautiful garden. Adam and Eve were to continue in the same manner, creating (procreating) and transforming the earth.

Bookstores are filled with titles on power, leadership, management, and creativity. Seminars on the same subjects, both Christian and secular, attract thousands of people. Within each person there is a creative passion that hungers to break free. We long to do something of significance, to discover a purpose for living that is beyond ourselves, to create something meaningful. I regularly receive phone calls and E-mail from people who share their desire to make a difference in the world. That encourages me, because I see that many people are looking for ways to exercise the creative power that God has given them. They are not content with what they are but are looking for what they might become.

As children, each of us has dreamed of what we will become, just as I did while riding the elevator at the department store. In our dreams there are no barriers. We have not yet been told we are of the wrong color, gender, size, or intellectual acumen. When we dream, we allow the creative power that God placed in our hearts to soar. When I speak with children especially, I find that they dream of becoming something quite noble.

Those dreams are clues to the blessing of God on our lives—the blessing of power. The equation of blessing to power may seem problematic, but it is not. Think of the many good uses of power. We know of the power of the Holy Spirit and the power of positive thinking. There is the power to heal and the power to forgive. There is power in leadership, and there is power in the truth. God entrusted Adam and Eve with the power to creatively manage the earth. He has entrusted that same power to you and me. We are blessed by the ability to create, to manage, to improve our world.

Yet power is not without danger. This very blessing can be corrupted to bring death rather than life, as God's first children soon discovered.

HOARDING POWER

The most significant observation about God's gift of power is perhaps the most obvious, though it is often overlooked. God created power in order to give it away. He did not maintain rigid control over his creation. Quite the opposite. He entrusted that power to his creation. We must assume, then, that Adam and Eve were likewise to share their power, to give it away. They were not to hoard power for themselves but were to entrust it to their offspring, just as God had done.

That life-giving plan was interrupted, however, when Adam and Eve succumbed to the temptation to hoard power. They yielded to the serpent's suggestion that they could make themselves "like God." Now we all struggle to understand difference between the blessing of true power and the curse of the corrupted power, the power of a lesser god.

One does not have to be a military leader, politician, or corporate CEO to realize that power must be used wisely. Each of us has a measure of power and may either give it away, as God intended, or hoard it for ourselves. I have wept many times after counseling sessions in which I'd heard a child recount the pain of being verbally abused or belittled by an angry parent. Likewise, I've often sympathized with parents who felt the shame of reacting to their own feelings of powerlessness by abusing their authority over their helpless children. I watched a promising executive become so consumed with the notion of personal power that he came to believe he was beyond accountability. Since those around him derived greater personal power by their association with him, they opposed any confrontation of his illegal and unethical behavior.

Even Jesus was tempted to abuse power. We know that Jesus is the creative force behind all of creation, yet when he took human form to walk the earth, he went through the same temptation as Adam and Eve. Jesus' temptation to power came during his time of fasting and praying in the desert. There, the devil took him to a high mountain and showed him all the kingdoms of the world and their splendor. Then the devil said, "All this I will give you if you bow down and worship me" (Matt. 4:8). Jesus' mission was to bring people back to God, but the question was how to do that. What would be his style of leadership? Would he be a conquering hero, which is what most people expected? Or would he use the power of love and sacrifice to win the world?

Ironically, this very temptation—to abuse power for personal gain—typified the very problem that Jesus had come to address. William Barclay has said that Christ's temptation was to come to terms with the world instead of uncompromisingly presenting God's demands to it. It was a temptation to try to change the world by becoming like it.[1] Jesus refused. He would not win the world by using the world's methods. Instead, he gave his power—indeed, his very life—away.

In his book, *In the Name of Jesus*, Henri Nouwen points out the rationalization that is often cited for misusing power. We figure that "as long as it is used in the service of God and your fellow human beings—it is a good thing."[2] Yet, Nouwen points out, this very rationalization is the foundation upon which many atrocities have been committed, including the crusades, the Inquisition, and human slavery. The temptation to misuse power is subtle. It is difficult to resist, Nouwen continues, beause it "offers an easy substitute for the hard task of love. It seems easier to be God than to love God, easier to control people than to love people, easier to own life than to love life."[3] It is easier to rule people than to love them. That is true at every level, from the nation to the family. Because it is so difficult to develop healthy, intimate relationships, we often chose power as a means of relating to one another.

As a parent of four active children, now adults, I was a soccer mom who spent a good deal of time at sporting events. That gave me the opportunity to observe coaches at every level of sport from Little League through collegiate athletics. I've noticed that there are two types of coaches in youth sports leagues. One type seems to have dreams of the big time but is never quite able to make it. This type of coach is obsessed with his or her own reputation and wants to win at any cost. Such coaches place a great deal of pressure on their eight- or ten-year-old athletes. Playing under the fear of punishment or humiliation, the children sometimes break, making errors that cost the game. Some simply quit, in despair of ever improving their skills or winning a game.

The second type of coach is one who wants the players to succeed. These coaches encourage their young charges, setting high expectations but equipping and encouraging the children to reach them. The greater skill of the children who played under such coaches was clearly evident, and they generally were winners.

What was the difference? One leader consumed power; the other gave it away. To achieve excellence is not, by itself, a blessing. To achieve excellence while building people at the same time, that is the blessing of power.

PERSONALIZING POWER

Cheryl Forbes, a journalist who for many years was an editor and writer for *Christianity Today*, authored the seminal book *The Religion of Power* in 1983. This fascinating work should have received much more attention than it did. The reason it did not have a greater impact, I believe, is that the Christian community at that time was too absorbed in the search for power and prestige to accept it. Perhaps that is still the case.

In her chapter "What Price Power?" Forbes observes that because we are blessed with power, we seem to believe that we can have whatever we want. She writes:

> If we want big churches, we can do it. We've got the power. Do we want money? Just follow these steps. We act as if God gave us a money-back guarantee with his command that we pray for our daily bread. . . . All that power is at our disposal; it is our "God-given mandate" to use it. God has become our Permissive Parent."[4]

Yet that is not the way God intended for his power to be used. Our tendency is to personalize power, to make it fit our needs. That is exactly opposite to the use of power that God gave to Adam and Eve. Their mandate was to give power away—to use it to benefit the world, not themselves. When power is personalized it becomes a consuming force. In this consumption, we do reckless and even wicked things in order to preserve and expand our own power.

One element of this personalization is the desire to be *named,* that is, to have others know who we are and what we have done. When we walk into a room, we like to be recognized. That may be one reason why politics has always interested me. My great aunt was definitely named by the people I admired. Even as a young person, that appealed to me; after all, everyone wants to be noticed. And in these days when everyone seems desperate to achieve fifteen minutes of fame, people are doing ridiculous and even dangerous things to be recognized.

It has been my experience on a number of occasions, and I admit that it feels good. I realize, too, that it is very dangerous. When you are a recognizable person, people name you beyond who you really are and have really done.

They do this because of their own desire for power. They can make the named person fit their own agenda.

The media are a ready tool for the personalization of power. I have seldom been on television, but World Hope International has produced several videos that have been widely distributed. I happen to appear in these videos in various scenes that have a tremendous emotional impact, such as holding starving babies in refugee camps. One Sunday, I was in the restroom of a church between morning services, and an awestruck teenage girl came up to me, asking for an autograph. "I've seen you on video," she said breathlessly. "You're that lady who travels all over the world." At that moment I realized the tremendous power of being named, especially in a visual medium.

I gave her the signature but talked with her about relief work, suggesting that she, too, could take part in assisting others. Yet I confess that I left the restroom thinking smugly, *I wonder just how many people do know me now?* This was the very temptation faced by Adam and Eve—the temptation to accept the power of a lesser god. I would face that temptation again a few weeks later.

Not long after the restroom incident, I was introduced at a speaking engagement, and as I listened to the introduction, I literally thought the host was speaking of someone else. The person he described was a superhuman; the introduction was just too good to be true. Yet it was flattering. As I took the few steps up to the podium, a battle took place in my mind. Should I embarrass the host by correcting him, or should I allow the exaggerated introduction to stand. Deep within me, it felt good to have the audience think that I was really that important. *At least they will be willing to listen to me,* I rationalized. *This may be a witness for Christ that will change someone's life.* In the end, I chose to clarify, kindly, some of the data that the host had presented.

Was it a small thing? Perhaps. Yet it was the same temptation that Jesus faced in the desert—to hoard power under the guise of doing good.

THE POWER TO GIVE LIFE

The blessing of power that God gave Adam and Eve is one that brings order out of chaos and life out of death. It is the power to work, to achieve, and to repair. There may be no more satisfying use of power than to mend a broken relationship. A few weeks ago, I saw that joy written on a young businessman's face as he sat in a prayer service. He reported to the group, "I have a great blessing for which I want to thank God. One of my colleagues and I had conflict and we were not able to work it out, but yesterday at a morning prayer meeting, we found our hearts brought together. I am so grateful." To mend broken relationships and develop intimate ones takes time, vulnerability, and, yes, the creative power of God. When it happens, I believe we see the true meaning of blessing.

I recently took part in organizational meetings for World Hope International in southern Africa. While there, I heard many stories of pain and death from South Africa, Mozambique, and Zambia. These countries have been long examples of the misuse of power. I wondered many times how southern Africa might be different today if the colonialists had practiced the concept of giving power rather than exploiting it. Although apartheid is no longer practiced as such, the mind-set that supported it continues to influence life in South Africa and Zambia; many beliefs and customs remain in place. As I drove past the walled compounds in Pretoria, the capital of South Africa, I noticed that the majority of the people waiting for public transportation were black. These were the workers who left their homes early in the morning to serve the upper and middle classes as domestic servants and returned late at night.

Breaking the beliefs and customs of power-holding groups does not come quickly or easily. Nelson Mandela and Desmond Tutu are two leaders who suffered much under Apartheid yet believed in the creative power of God to heal a nation. Nelson Mandela spent twenty-seven years in a rat-infested prison but never gave up the vision of hope and dignity for every person in South Africa. Desmond Tutu, the Anglican Archbishop Emeritus of Cape Town, South Africa, suffered personally at the hands of powerful leaders yet believed that forgiveness and reconciliation could bring a nation together.

Tutu initiated the Truth and Reconciliation Commission in 1995, which allowed people from all sides of the conflict to confess their involvement in political violence and receive amnesty. The result has been an incredible level of healing in that country. His book, *No Future without Forgiveness*, outlines the details of this process. He tells of the long awaited day, April 27, 1994, when at the age of sixty-two, he voted for the first time. Nelson Mandela was seventy-six.

The model of healing a nation through truth and reconciliation started in South Africa has begun in many countries of the world. Others are using the concept of giving away power in order to bring healing to their communities. Desmond Tutu concludes, "Our experiment is going to succeed because God wants us to succeed, not for our glory and aggrandizement but for the sake of God's world. God wants to show that there is life after conflict and repression—that because of forgiveness there is a future."[5]

As I think about my own nation, my own community— indeed my own life—I must wonder which conflicts might have been avoided if we had not been so eager to hoard power, and which might be healed if we were more willing to give power away.

POWER VERSUS POSITION

Power is a blessing from God, and we, his children, possess it. We are generally confused about the nature of power, however, and often mistake it for position. As a result, we complain of our powerlessness while we maneuver to get into a position to exercise the power we think should be ours.

Yet if power is essentially life giving, we can exercise power wherever we are by giving life to others.

Lisa is an example of giving life without having a position of authority. Lisa worked with InterVarsity Christian Fellowship in Odessa, Ukraine. While sharing her faith with university students, she became aware of the growing numbers of children who lived on the street. Lisa inquired into the state of these children, but could find no private or government agency that was caring for them. Her passion grew. One cold, winter day she discovered sixty children living in the sewers near her apartment, for warmth. Lisa's passion became fire, and a conviction formed in her mind. *I must do something about this,* she resolved. Today, Lisa ministers to hundreds of children in Odessa. She has assembled a very able support staff, but she still prefers to work directly with the children. Position means little to Lisa. She has found that real power comes through intimacy.

Congregations as well as individuals can exercise life-giving power, yet many churches feel that they are powerless under the evil in their communities. That is because they define power in terms of money, influence, personnel, and resources. None of those elements are prerequisites for the blessing of power that God wants us to bestow.

Many years ago, I shared a concern about gang violence with the women's ministries board of a church in suburban St. Louis, Missouri. As clinical director for a community mental health center, I had attended a meeting in the inner city regarding increased gang activity in the suburbs. The attorney for juvenile offenders who made the presentation was a passionate speaker. At one point, she displayed a map of the area with certain neighborhoods circled in red. My own community of Warrenton, Missouri, had the largest red circle on the entire map. I was stunned. We had been known as a safe, family-friendly community.

When I asked for more information, the presenter said, "This community has been targeted by the Crips and the

Bloods from Chicago. They see it strategic because it is located on Interstate 70, and they also think they will find a lot of kids who long for the 'tough' life."

Three days later I repeated that information to the women's ministry board. I barely had the words out of my mouth when one of the ten women said, "We must do something to stop this." Others nodded their heads in agreement. These were not women with positions of influence or great wealth, but they were ready to give their power to bring the blessing of life to a community. We started by holding an informational breakfast and inviting various community leaders. I was assigned to invite the fiery attorney as the speaker.

On the morning of the breakfast, it was standing room only in the banquet room of the Wagon Wheel Restaurant. Every level of the community was represented. The attorney began her presentation by directing attention to a semi-trailer that was parked across the street. I'm not sure who owned the trailer, but it had been parked there for months, and graffiti was scrawled all along the side. The attorney began to "read" the graffiti to us and explained that the symbols were insignia of various gangs, who were operating in our neighborhood already. She definitely had the crowd's attention!

After that meeting, the church women organized follow-up sessions with strategic community leaders to form an action plan. As a result, the Crips and Bloods were unable to get a foothold. They soon abandoned their plan and went elsewhere. This tiny group of women who had no position exercised life-giving power on behalf of an entire community. Based on that experience, one of the women ran for a seat on the school board and was elected. She continued to exercise life-giving power from that position.

Ironically, many people who jostle for positions of power discover that, once the position is obtained, they are actually less effective than before. In the same way, some leaders find that they have greater influence after surrendering power.

Former President Jimmy Carter illustrates that phenomenon. His efforts to bring peace and reconciliation around the world have been far more effective as a private citizen than they were when he was president of the most powerful nation on earth. He was awarded the Nobel Peace Prize in 2002, more than twenty years after he left office. The positions that we seek as a means to power are often unnecessary. God has already given us the power to change the world.

USING THE GIFT

God gave the blessing of power at Creation, and Jesus affirmed it in the Last Supper. There, Christ took two basic elements of human existence, bread and wine, and breathed into them his transforming presence. Through his sacrifice, it is possible for human beings once again to enjoy union with our Creator. His body is our bread, the source from which we receive the life-giving power to create and to love others. His blood is our wine, which strengthens and energizes our hearts so that we may give life to our brothers and sisters. The Last Supper, then, is more than a simple ritual. In it we receive the life-giving body and blood of our Lord and pass that blessing on to one another. Cheryl Forbes sums it up eloquently:

> To show our thankfulness, we pass his power among as many as we can. This is the proper progression: the manifestation of his power—the gift; the disciplined gratitude for that gift—the receiving; the sharing of the power—the giving away and worship; and the godly receive of the power back to himself. This true Power is not ours to keep but only ours to accept and quickly give to someone else. We don't own it; we have no right to it. It is a grant gladly given from its Source. And only for a time.[6]

The sacrifice of Jesus' body and blood led to his resurrection from the dead. That Resurrection continues today as lives, relationships, and even organizations are transformed by Jesus' life-giving power. We enjoy the blessing of God when we share that power with the world. I often wonder what might be possible if we fully appreciated—and rightly used—the awesome power that God has given to us.

In her book *Teaching a Stone to Talk,* Annie Dillard captured my imagination with her description of God's power as something that will "draw us out to where we can never return." She reminds us that the power God wants to reveal in us is truly world changing. Dillard asks:

> Does anyone have the foggiest idea what sort of power we so blithely invoke? Or, as I suspect, does one not believe a word of it? The churches are playing on the floor with their chemistry sets, mixing up a batch of TNT to kill a Sunday morning. It is madness to wear ladies' straw hats and velvet hats to church; we should all be wearing crash helmets. Ushers should issue life preservers and signal flares; they should lash us to our pews. For the sleeping god may wake and take offense, or the waking god may draw us out to where we can never return.[7]

What will be the result in your life when you accept the blessing of power that God has for you? What will be the result in your community when you give that power away? God only knows.

TO THINK ABOUT

1. List some situations in which you have power. In which
   have you used power selfishly? In which have you used
   power to give life?

2. Give two examples of occasions when you felt powerless.

3. In what ways could you empower someone else?

4. If you fully realized the blessing of power that God has
   for you, what do you think your life would look like?

THE BLESSING
OF HOLINESS

*The road to holiness necessarily passes
through the world of action.*
—Dag Hammarskjold

I n the late 1960s, I worked in a welfare program that had
the noble aim of revitalizing our decaying cities. The
overall program, known as the Great Society, had been
created by President Lyndon Johnson and included a feder-
ally funded grassroots effort known as the War on Poverty.
The particular program I directed in Kansas City, Missouri,
had the aim of helping people move from poverty into
productive careers. We were not interested merely in placing
people in low-end jobs with no opportunity for advance-
ment. We had contracted with various agencies to provide
the education and training that would place our clients on
genuine career paths.

I always find it amusing to read articles on the failure of
the Great Society, since I know of many people whose
lives—and whose descendants' lives—have been forever

changed because of the opportunities afforded them in those days. At one point I did a financial analysis of the five hundred people with whom we had worked, comparing the amount they now paid in taxes to the amount of welfare support they had received. I found that in two years, the taxes they paid to the government would equal the amount they had received from the government in the previous year.

During that time, my husband, Wayne, was attending a seminary that emphasized the need for holy living. We believed—and do believe—that to be holy means to be set apart, dedicated to God for a special purpose. Wayne also served as pastor at a small church in the inner city, which held the same view. In our ecclesiastical circles, the War on Poverty was much derided. Many times we were asked when we would sell the church's property and relocate the congregation to a better neighborhood. The concept of holy living, as I understood it at that time, had little or nothing to do with engaging the world. In fact, it was just the opposite. To be holy was to be separate from the world—set apart.

Each day, I gave my energy to serving the people with whom I worked, but I really didn't see that as part of my religious life. My work had nothing to do with my faith. My life was compartmentalized. At that time, my dream of being "blessed" was to live in the suburbs, with Wayne as pastor of an upscale church that had a parking lot filled with expensive cars.

Yet I was torn. Even as I longed for a comfortable suburban life, I sensed that God was pulling me toward the world in which I was serving. How could that be? The religious circles in which I moved would never affirm working in an inner-city welfare program as living a holy life. Holy living was always defined in personal terms. Holy people read their Bibles, prayed every day, and scrupulously avoided sin. They set themselves apart from the very sort of people I was drawn toward. Justice, poverty, and other social concerns were rarely thought of in connection with holiness.

What does it mean to be holy? I wondered. *And what does God want me to do with my life?*

BLESSING AS HOLINESS

A catalytic moment came in the spring of 1969. I had been greatly pleased with the progress of one woman in our program, whom I'll call Mary. Mary was a second-generation welfare recipient and the mother of five children. She lived in the housing projects. Through an opportunity presented by our program, Mary had obtained her high school equivalency diploma and enrolled in a community college to study accounting. Eventually, Mary got a job as a bookkeeper with the municipal housing authority. She received additional assistance for child care and transportation, which enabled her to continue both working and going to school. She seemed to be doing fine.

Yet every week, Mary requested an advance on her funds for the next week. During a group counseling session, she revealed the reason. Every payday, Mary's boyfriend came to her house and demanded money. Not having the strength to resist him, she would hand over the majority of her earnings every two weeks. We later discovered that she would buy only one quart of milk at a time because she did not have a refrigerator.

The women in the support group began to encourage Mary to resist "her man." They all gave examples of times when they'd had to do the same. Mary left that day with a new resolve to gain her freedom. On her way out, she stopped by my office to tell me of her plans. I watched her walk down the steps, head held high, a determined air about her, eyes sparkling with hope. Deep inside, I wanted to take her and her five children home with me that night to protect them from what I feared would take place.

At ten o'clock the next morning, my office phone rang.

The weak voice on the line was Mary's. "Mrs. Lyon, I tried to do what I planned, but my boyfriend beat me. Can someone help me?" One of our follow-up coaches was dispatched to Mary's apartment immediately. There, she found Mary covered with bruises and abrasions. An examination revealed that Mary's ribs were broken; she was admitted to the hospital.

My heart broke that day. A thousand questions flooded my mind. Why did this have to happen? Why couldn't her boyfriend rejoice at Mary's success? I could guess the answer to that, but a deeper question continued to haunt me. Where was God? Why didn't he protect her? That night at church, we prayed for Mary. Throughout the night, I alternately questioned God and prayed for his protection of Mary. *Where will it end?* I wondered. In my heart, I knew the answer.

After a brief hospital stay, Mary was released and went home. Her doctor suggested that she stay home for a week before returning to work and school. Our coaches made regular visits and reported that Mary was recovering nicely. Then on Monday, Mary did not return to work as scheduled. Fearing the worst, I sent a follow-up coach to her home. An hour later, we heard the awful report. Mary had been beaten to death by her boyfriend. Now the question of God's protection returned to my mind even stronger than before, but this time there was a twist—I accused myself with the same question. *Why weren't you there when she needed you?*

The seminary my husband attended held a monthly meeting for the spouses of students. A meeting was scheduled for that evening, the very day that I'd received the news of Mary's death. At first I thought to skip the meeting but then decided to go, thinking that there I might find some answer to the questions that weighed upon my soul. I left for the meeting immediately after work.

As I entered the meeting room, I saw a big wedding cake on a graciously appointed table. It was a beautiful sight, and that was certainly welcome. As I took my seat, I noticed that several other tables were decorated differently. Soon, the meeting began and the theme was announced. This meeting would be devoted to two subjects: how to cut a wedding cake and how to entertain the district superintendent. I stared blankly as the presenters spoke, explaining the finer points of cake cutting, sandwich making, and tea pouring. Images of what I imagined Mary and her children had endured flashed before my eyes. Would Mary have been offended if I hadn't known how to cut a wedding cake? Would she have cared whether I served from the right or cleared from the left? Would she have known what a district superintendent was? Would she have cared?

I spoke to no one as I left the meeting; I realized that none of them would have any idea what I'd experienced that day, and I was too exhausted to tell them. I started the engine of my little blue Volkswagen and drove home through a flood of tears. As I crashed through the door of our house, I cried out to Wayne, "Where is God? Where is the Church? People are dying in the streets and all they want me to do is cut wedding cakes."

That was the first time I'd given voice to these disturbing questions about the nature of God and the holy life. Having finally summoned the courage to speak the words aloud, renewed faith began to grow in my heart. In the days that followed, I began to make a spiritual discovery. I wondered, *If the life that God blesses is a life that is set apart, could that include being set apart to live amid the pain and suffering of the world, set apart to make a difference?*

In fact, that is precisely what it does mean to be set apart. It means being fully engaged in the world, not removed from it. Jesus prayed for his disciples not that they would be taken out of the world but that they would be protected from evil while in it (John 17:15). We are set apart by God for a purpose, to redeem the world by his love. When I finally grasped the idea that being set apart is an active and not a passive thing, a sense of God's peace came over my soul.

THE MEANING OF HOLINESS

The word *bless*, in various forms, appears more than five hundred times in the Bible. There are at least six meanings for this word, including to confer happiness, to grant favor, and to praise or glorify. The first meaning, however, is this one: to set apart and make holy.[1] That is the meaning of *blessed* as it is used in Gen. 2:3. There we read that "God blessed the seventh day and hallowed it, because on it God rested from all the work that he had done in creation."

To our twenty-first-century minds, being set apart sounds, well, dull. The word *holy* sounds worse—churchy, sentimental, out of touch. Yet holiness is a dynamic concept. God doesn't set people apart for no reason. He sanctifies people (makes them holy) for a purpose. When we are blessed by God, we are singled out for a reason, a purpose, a mission. Although I was raised in a Christian home, it took me nearly twenty-five years to discover that. The journey began in a small town in north central Oklahoma.

MY JOURNEY TO HOLINESS

Both my mother and father were preachers. Each had great passion to see others come to faith in Christ. In fact, I was born during a tent revival they conducted in Blackwell, Oklahoma. From that series of revival meetings, a church was organized and a building constructed. The congregation grew in number as my parents, particularly my mother, reached into that depressed community, making converts by caring for, visiting, and nurturing the people. My father was an administrator and visionary who helped organize a number of other churches in that region.

I have a vivid memory of accompanying my mother one day as she went "calling," which meant visiting people's homes. Because she intended to cover a lot of ground that afternoon, my mother placed me in a baby buggy. I was too old—and too big—to be pushed in a stroller, but my mother knew that I wouldn't be able to keep up on foot. So for several hours, I rode through the streets of Blackwell as my mother boldly knocked on doors and cheerfully invited people to church.

AWAKENING PASSION

A few years later, our family moved to Enid, Oklahoma, where my parents continued the same pattern of ministry. There was one woman of color who came to our neighborhood though. Early on Wednesday mornings, a sturdy African-American woman would make her way down our modest, bungalow-lined street and collect the trash we had put at the curb, heaving it into the back of a pickup truck. The clatter of the trash cans seemed to match the rhythm of her singing, and this strong woman greatly intrigued me. I would run to press my nose against the windowpane just to get a closer look at her.

One day, I asked my father where she lived. He explained that she lived in "Colored Town." I was filled with questions about this place, and to answer them, my father said, "Would you like to go see where she lives?" As a five-year-old, I was delighted and curious at the prospect. I raced to the car, and Dad drove us to the area of town inhabited by people of color. I was stunned by what I saw. The pavement ended at the edge of "colored town," where tar-paper shacks seemed to be the primary form of building. There was a pungent smell from meat being cooked in several small restaurants. There were stores, and other businesses, and houses—it was an entire town. I'd had no idea that such a place existed in our community.

I asked my father many questions about that experience, including this one: "Why don't those people come to our church?" His answer was equivocal. I didn't fully understand

71

why people lived in that place or why we didn't invite them to our church. I did, however, sense the beginning of a desire that would grow in me over time—a desire to make things better. For years after that, whenever our family traveled through a new city, I would beg them to take me through "the slums." Even then, I longed for something more than simply to follow the rules and be nice; I felt set apart by God for something more. At that young age, I did not know that what I hungered for was a holy life—a life of meaning and purpose.

GROWING DISSATISFACTION

After graduating from high school, I attended a secular university. There I was free to question the cultural restrictions imposed by my church. Our church interpreted the idea of being set apart to mean being disengaged from the fashion, entertainment, and lifestyle of the world. During my university years, I questioned those views but would not risk the disapproval of the church community by openly disengaging from them.

After graduation from college, I married Wayne, whom I'd met as a senior in high school. He was called to the ministry, which meant that my life from then on would be more or less the same as my parents' had been. I knew what that would be like. We would serve within the same denomination in which I'd been raised, and I would find my identity through Wayne and his church career. Although our denomination was the first to ordain a woman in America and had once been very encouraging of women in ministry, by the 1960s it had very few female ministers, and a number of church leaders were outspoken critics of the ordination of women. Actually, that bothered me little at that time because I didn't envision myself in any leadership role. I thought I would simply be a pastor's wife.

In 1963 we moved to our first church assignment in Springfield, Missouri. The congregation was small but had a new church building and a lovely, brick bungalow parsonage.

The church had not had a pastor for a year, and things were not going well. The congregation had dwindled to about twenty-five people, and there were only two children in the Sunday school. The new building offered excellent Sunday school rooms, however, and there was one large room that was well suited for children's church. My enthusiasm welled as I cleaned those rooms, decorated the bulletin boards, and envisioned a church filled with children. One of the members of the congregation saw that Wayne and I were working at the church and stopped by to see what was happening. When I showed him my accomplishment, he said, "Why are you doing all this work? We only have two kids?"

Yet my enthusiasm would not be dampened. "We're going to fill this place," I responded.

He looked at me as if I had lost my mind, shrugged his shoulders, and walked away.

I wish I could report that this enthusiasm was long term. It wasn't. Although the Sunday school rooms were soon bustling with children and new families filled the church sanctuary, I felt empty. I quickly grew tired of the routine, I no longer looked forward to going to church, and I didn't want to be around people. The role of pastor's wife had lost its charm; I hungered for something more.

But what?

CONFRONTATION

Perhaps it was new clothes. Perhaps it was a redecorated parsonage. Perhaps it was better health. Perhaps it was a better marriage. Perhaps I would be happy if my husband weren't a pastor. I tried to satisfy my inner longing in all of those ways—buying new clothes and new curtains, dieting, reading books on improving marriage. Finally I arrived at what seemed the only road left: I asked my husband to leave the ministry.

Naturally, I couched my request in the noblest of terms. "Wayne," I said softly, "you have such a great personality.

Have you ever thought of how much money you could make as an insurance salesman? Why, if you doubled your income, think of the money we could give to the poor."

He looked at me narrowly. "What are you talking about?"

As I explained more of my plan, I saw the resolve in his piercing blue eyes. "Jo Anne," he said slowly, "I don't know what you are going to do, but God has called me to preach, and that is what I'm going to do." I realized then that this man truly believed the words of Jesus, "Seek first the Kingdom of God and His righteousness and all these things will be added unto you" (Matt. 6:33).

A month or so later, I arrived home from teaching school on a cold December day and began to prepare supper. I was washing my hands in the sink when I sensed a nearly audible voice, which I knew was from God. *Jo Anne, you need to get your spiritual life straightened out.*

Me, I questioned. *What are you talking about? I read the Bible and pray every morning.* I picked up a potato and began to peel, still arguing in my mind. *Well, maybe I do need to change, but it will have to wait. Right now I'm busy with the Christmas program, and then in February there's the. . . .*

I listed my excuses, but in my heart, I knew that I longed for something more. Could that something be God? How could that be true? I had been a believer my whole life. Didn't our church have a corner on the idea of holy living? Why then was I so miserably unhappy? I was living as God wanted me to—wasn't I?

A few days later, Wayne and I were putting up a Christmas tree in our house. We began to bicker over the placement of the tree, then over the lights, and before long we had a full-blown argument. Finally, I'd had it. I couldn't stand to live with the unresolved tension in my heart—and between Wayne and me. I marched into the bedroom, packed my bags, loaded them into the car, and drove away, planning never to return.

For an hour or so, I drove aimlessly around town trying

to decide what to do. I really had no place to go. I couldn't go to a church member's home because I didn't want anyone to know that Wayne and I were fighting. My nearest family members were eight hundred miles away. I checked my purse and found that I had all of two dollars in cash. In those days before automatic teller machines, I had no choice but to wait until the bank opened the next morning. I planned to withdraw some money and drive to my parents' home in Ohio, but first I needed to find a safe street where I could park the car and sleep. I had just rounded a corner about two blocks from our house when the front of the car plunged down and the vehicle jerked to a halt. A road crew had been making repairs and left a gaping hole in the pavement. The car was buried up to the axle. I would have to find a phone, call a garage, and get the car towed—all with just two dollars. Under the circumstances, I had little choice but to return home.

I would like to say that when I arrived, Wayne and I fell into each other's arms, asked forgiveness, and were blissfully reunited, but that doesn't describe either one of us. We were both stubborn. I retreated to one bedroom and he to the other. We lived that way for weeks.

UNEXPECTED BLESSING

Some time later, I awoke one morning desperately ill. I had terrible pain in my stomach, and couldn't keep from vomiting. Between trips to the bathroom, I lay face down on the floor, the only comfortable position I could find. Returning from an early-morning prayer meeting at the church, Wayne discovered my condition and realized it was more serious than a normal case of the flu. He scooped me up from the floor and took me to the emergency room of the hospital. I was admitted into the intensive care unit, and doctors began tests to diagnose my problem.

As I lay on the gurney being wheeled up to the intensive care unit, I thought, *Well, Lord, I guess you must have me in here so I can be a witness to someone.* Even in my distress,

I believed that I was still in a superior position to those around me. That was the result of my spiritual training, even though I was trying to run from it. Immediately, the words of an old spiritual came to my mind, "It's not my brother or my sister but it's me, O Lord, standing in the need of prayer." I knew it was true. My body had been crushed under the weight of the spiritual burden that I carried. I needed to change, and I knew it. I was finally ready.

When Wayne was allowed to visit, I shocked him with a request. I asked that he bring a book to me that he had been urging me to read. I had resisted reading it partly because it was he who had suggested it and partly because I believed that I knew all there was to know about being a Christian. The next day Wayne brought the book, *Beyond Ourselves* by Catherine Marshall, and I opened it eagerly.

My eyes fell first upon the chapter entitled "Ego Slaying." I found that surprising because I thought the notion of self-sacrifice was peculiar to my own tradition. Here was a Presbyterian, no less, writing about the need to surrender oneself. I quickly turned to that chapter and began to read. I saw my entire life reflected in Catherine Marshall's words. What's more, they created in me an insatiable hunger to know God more.

There had been an unexplained change in my stomach acids, and my illness went away. I was released from the hospital a short time later. I believe that God did "surgery" on my heart, and therefore I didn't need surgery on my stomach. Something had changed in me both spiritually and physically. I came to realize that I had been trying to live with a divided heart. Over the next few days, I began to confess selfish attitudes to God. With each confession, I gained a greater sense of his presence and greater peace within. I realized that I could be completely honest with God and that as I was more honest with him, the distance between us was reduced.

One Wednesday evening in late January, about twenty people had gathered at our church for the usual midweek prayer service. Everyone knew the routine: we would sing a few hymns, mention some prayer requests, have a brief Bible study, and pray. As the service began, we sang an old gospel song I had sung many times before. I had probably memorized the lyrics, having sung them so much, but I never paid close attention to the words until that night.

> All my lifelong I had panted
>   For a drink from some cool spring
> That I thought would quench the burning
>   Of the thirst I felt within.
> Hallelujah! I have found Him—
>   Whom my soul so long has craved!
> Jesus satisfies my longings;
>   Thro' His blood I now am saved.[2]

Suddenly I rose to my feet and confessed to the people all of the things I had struggled with over the past few months—my dread of coming to church, my dislike for them, and my attempt to run away. With tears streaming down my face, I told them of the overwhelming love I now felt for them. This love was truly a gift—a blessing—from God. It was not a fleeting emotional experience; it became the doorway to a new path, one that I walked daily with Jesus.

For me, life had become an adventure, an adventure of holy living. I had learned that being set apart really meant being thrust into action in God's world, not alone, but with the power of the Holy Spirit. I began to identify with those people mentioned in the book of Acts who had been waiting for something after the ascension of Jesus. When the Holy Spirit descended upon them, they were filled with boldness and courage, and they began to see those around them through the compassionate eyes of Jesus. I felt the same. For the first time in my life, I began to see my world not with disdain or pity, but with hope.

HOLINESS AND BLESSING

What is the evidence that one has been filled with the Holy Spirit? That question has been the subject of debate for centuries, and there has been a wide range of answers. Some, like the ancient desert fathers, have considered a holy (meaning ascetic) lifestyle to be the evidence of God's presence within. Others, notably modern Pentecostals, have held that speaking in an unknown language is the sign of God's blessing. In either case, the focus of attention is often placed on the evidence of God's presence rather than on God himself.

My own tradition has often used the term *second blessing* to describe the indwelling of the Holy Spirit. The first blessing is salvation—the forgiveness of sins that begins a believer's walk with God. The second blessing is the moment, described in the book of Acts, when the Holy Spirit comes to reside within the person. It is worth noting that in both cases, the term *blessing* describes the imparting of righteousness to us by God. Neither forgiveness nor holiness is a gift we can give to ourselves.

But how does all of that affect our daily lives? Regardless of how the Holy Spirit comes to us, what is the result of his presence in us? Two young friends of mine provide a stellar answer.

Sherry and Dave Herter relocated to the outer suburbs of St. Louis in 1977. They both enjoyed having a little more space, and the location afforded Dave many opportunities to pursue his hobbies of hunting and fishing. Sherry, however, was not able to find a position as an administrative assistant, her previous line of work. She finally settled for a factory job at a company that manufactured hospital beds. The work was fast paced and very hard, seeming to match the lifestyle of her coworkers. Each person had a radio blaring to break the monotony and boredom of the job. Many of the workers smoked marijuana, sometimes on the job, to relieve the tension in their lives. Foul language was heard constantly. Sherry saw her soft hands become callused and wondered why God hadn't blessed her with a better job.

Dave and Sherry had always attended church but had never understood what it meant to be filled with the Holy Spirit—set apart by God to live a holy life. Gradually, the hunger for something more began to grow within them. It wasn't long before God met their hunger with His Spirit. Sherry's attitude about her job soon changed. She began to see that God had placed her there—set her apart—amid that rough and rowdy group of people.

With that new attitude, Sherry began to listen to her coworkers. When they saw that she was responsive to them, they began to share some of the details of their torn and tattered lives. Sherry started a Bible study at the factory, and many of her coworkers began to attend church. I will never forget the women's retreats to which Sherry brought eight or ten women from the factory. For most of them, attending the retreat was their first experience at connecting with God; several became Christians.

Sometime later Sherry was offered an administrative position with a Christian organization. She turned it down. "A couple of years ago," she said, "working for that ministry would have been my dream job. But I can't accept it now. I need to stay at the factory—this is my ministry."

God did not simply tell us to be holy as he is holy. He demonstrated that holiness by sending his Son, Jesus, into the rough and tumble of human life. It is there, amid the people, problems, and pressures of the world, that holiness must be put into practice.

Dag Hammarskjold, secretary general of the United Nations from 1953 to 1961, has been described as a man in whom the active, outer life and the contemplative, inner life meet. In his book *Markings,* Hammarskjold writes of his desire to live a holy life. At the end of 1954, a tumultuous international year, he penned an affirmation of faith which showed his desire to be both pure on the inside and active in the world on the outside.

> Give me a pure heart—that I may see Thee, a humble heart—that I may hear Thee, a heart of love—that I may serve Thee. A heart of faith—that I may abide in Thee.[3]

A few days later, he wrote what may be the theme for his entire life's work: "In our era, the road to holiness necessarily passes through the world of action."[4]

That has certainly been true of me. Since my own defining moment in Springfield, Missouri, my journey has taken me through the world of action. The action has not always been breathtaking, world changing, or exhilarating. It has often consisted of boring days, tiring tasks, and feelings of uselessness. Yet underlying every day of my journey has been the realization that God has called me into a relationship not only with my own family and friends but also with strangers, scattered across the face of the earth. I have been set apart for a purpose, and I find joy in fulfilling it. For it is in living our purpose that we discover the true meaning of being blessed.

Henri Nouwen has written a prayer entitled "A Preacher's Prayer," which ends with a petition that resonates with my desire to complete this journey into holiness.

> Do not allow evil powers to seduce me with the complexities of the world's problems, but give me the strength to think clearly, speak freely, and act boldly in your service. Give me the courage to show the dove in a world so full of serpents. Amen.[5]

Truly, we live in a world of serpents—a complex and challenging place. Yet we are set apart for a purpose: to redeem the world through the love of Jesus Christ. Let us be engaged in that work—set apart to be holy, set apart for a purpose. For that is the meaning of being holy as God is holy.

TO THINK ABOUT

1. When you hear the word holy, what comes to mind?

2. Describe a time in your life when you had great hunger for God.

3. Have you been filled with the Holy Spirit? How do you know?

4. What is the issue, problem, or situation in your community that most arouses your passion?

5. How might the world be different if holy people took the issues of racial reconciliation, sex trafficking, hunger, AIDS, or the environment more seriously?

CHAPTER FOUR

The Blessing
of Loss

*The moment I let go of it was the moment
I got more than I could handle.*
—Alanis Morrissette, "Thank U"

The obstetrician walked into the examining room where I
sat anxiously awaiting his verdict. He rapped on the
wooden door for emphasis and said, "You're as sterile as this
wooden door. You might as well go into the world and produce
other things because you will never produce children."

Those were not the words I'd hoped to hear. After years
of being unable to conceive, I'd submitted to the long and
arduous routine of a fertility workup. I was hoping desperately for some good news, some ray of hope, even a slim
chance that I might one day conceive. I left the doctor's
office in a daze and drove back to my job at the social services agency in the inner city of Kansas City, Missouri. Sitting
at my desk, I mused, *Well, I guess this is the place where
God wants me to give life.*

That was a brave front, but I wasn't sure it would last.

Often, when I receive discouraging news, my faith is strong at the outset but weakens as I wrestle with the changes that follow. I wanted to see my situation as a blessing, but how? We usually think of a blessing as something that is received, not as something denied or taken away. How could I find God in what seemed a totally negative experience—the inability to bear children?

I could not have known it then, but on that day I began to experience God's blessing in one of its most unlikely forms—loss. For God often chooses to bless us not with what we have but with what we do not have and even what we must surrender.

BLESSING AS LETTING GO

I did not enjoy being childless, and the bold, usually unwelcome comments I received were no help in accepting my situation. I now find it merely astounding, but at the time it was infuriating when people would ask intrusive questions such as "Whose fault is it?" or say with a wink and a smile, "What's the matter? Don't you know how to do it?" Others would presume to offer advice, saying, "You had better forget that education and start having a family or you'll soon be too old." I would return such remarks with a polite smile, but I felt as if I were always the butt of some joke. I was embarrassed about my infertility, and angry. But I coped with it well, I thought, throwing my energy into pursuing an education and my social work in the inner city.

One Sunday morning, several years after the doctor had pronounced me as sterile as a wooden door, I was sitting in the second row at the small inner-city church where my husband, Wayne, was pastor. He was performing the ritual of dedication for a beautiful baby, the child of a lovely young couple in the church. The entire congregation was celebrating the birth of this baby, and I joined in that affirmation of life. Suddenly, tears began to well in my eyes, and I began to feel an emotion I could not describe. Into my consciousness came these words: *You have resentment in your heart because you do not have a baby.*

No, I told myself emphatically, *that's not true.* For years, I had taken pride in the manner in which I'd accepted my barrenness. *I've accepted this,* I thought. *I'm beyond it. I'm doing other good things with my life.* Yet the words lingered in my spirit, and I realized that there was truth in them. I had suppressed my feelings of anger. Underneath the cool exterior that I'd tried to project, I grieved the loss of children I would never hold. But what could I do with these feelings now?

Almost immediately, I realized it was the Holy Spirit who had spoken to me. When we live in his immediate presence, he lets us know when actions, attitudes, or desires of our heart are out of sync with his will. As I opened my heart to this revelation, I began to see what might lie ahead of me if I did not change. Over time, unconfessed resentment could become bitterness; bitterness might change to malice; and malice to hatred. Hatred—that is the destination of the journey that begins with the simple act of harboring resentment over a loss. In that state, it is impossible to live a life of energy, purpose, and meaning. Too much emotional energy must be consumed in keeping the hate alive. In an instant, I saw what my life might become if I did not deal with those feelings.

As I sat in the pew that morning, I confessed to the Lord the resentment I held against him for having denied me the privilege of bearing children. As I saw it, I had two choices for the future. I could either *relinquish* my infertility or *resign* myself to it. The difference between the two is subtle but powerful. I picture it this way: to relinquish a circumstance is to approach God with an open hand, saying, "Here it is, Lord. I don't know what to do with this, but I look forward to what you will do." Relinquishment is not an attempt to second-guess God or to manipulate him. It is an act of willing surrender. To resign, on the other hand, is to approach God with a closed hand—a fist—saying, "If this is the way life has to be, then I'll grit my teeth and bear it. I'll accept this thing, but nothing on earth will ever make me like it." Resignation accepts the circumstance but stubbornly resists God in the process.

Somehow, I chose to relinquish my infertility that morning. I opened my hand and let God take the burden of resentment away from me. In the days that followed, I experienced great peace and freedom in my spirit. I really didn't know what God was going to do or if he would do anything, but I trusted him to do what was best for me. For the first time, I began to understand the feeling of the psalm writers, who so often express their complete trust in almighty God.

Relinquishment changes the focus of one's energy. The focus moves from the good thing that God might provide (in my case, fertility) to God himself. Afterward, a sense of peace results from believing that God will do something good through the situation. The key to maintaining that peace is to trust God and not try to direct him. Peace comes from anticipating God's creative work, whatever that might be.

I have seen prayers of relinquishment that were answered in precisely opposite ways. For example, I've known a number of people who have been separated from their spouse during a troubled marriage and have relinquished the situation to God. In some cases, the estranged partner returned and the two were reconciled. In other cases, the spouse did not return, yet the one who had relinquished the marriage to God experienced a marvelous sense of peace. Relinquishment does not prescribe what action God must take; rather, it opens us to receive his blessing, whatever it may be.

Relinquishment is really a journey. I made the decision to relinquish my situation to God on a single Sunday morning, but it took months to work that acceptance into all of my attitudes and actions. With each day, my sense of surrender and my willingness to trust God grew. My sense of peace and contentment grew as well.

Often, the act of giving something up to God must be accompanied by action. For example, I have counseled people who struggled with addictions of various kinds and could only fully surrender to God by doing something active. One man in particular was addicted to pornography. Although he was a Christian, he had struggled secretly with this obsession for years. The act of openly seeking help for his problem was an important step in relinquishing it. When we give up something, it may need to be replaced by something else. That requires actively changing habits and patterns of behavior.

Sitting in the doctor's office all those years ago, I would never have believed that infertility could somehow be God's blessing upon me. It was, but only after I learned to let it go. Little did I realize that God had still more blessings in mind for me—some quite different from what I'd expected.

BLESSING AS CLEANSING

Several months prior to my "relinquishment day," Wayne and I had applied to a adoption social service agency in hopes of adopting a child. Everything went like clockwork. We filled out all the required paperwork, and the social worker did a home study and completed all the necessary information; everything was in order. Our caseworker called excitedly one morning to say that we should be ready to appear in court the next day. It appeared that we were about to become the adoptive parents of a baby boy. All we knew about him was that he had dark hair, but that was more than enough to get us excited. Wayne and I were up early the next morning, eagerly awaiting the phone call. After what seemed like hours of nervously pacing the floor, the phone rang. Wayne answered immediately, and almost as quickly, I could tell something was wrong. After a brief and somber conversation, he hung up the phone and turned around, disappointment evident on his face. "The judge has changed his mind," Wayne said softly. "He decided to award this baby to someone else— a couple that already has children."

"Why?" I asked in disbelief. "Why would he do that to us?"

Wayne explained: "It seems that the judge grew up as an only child. He thinks it would be better for this baby to be given to a family that already has children rather than to be placed with us—alone."

I sat there in stunned silence. After awhile I thought, *Oh well. There will be another. I'm sure we'll have another opportunity soon.* But we didn't. For months we received no communication from the adoption agency. Desperate to keep involved in the process, I began to call the social worker regularly. I was determined to make something happen.

After my relinquishment day, however, I just stopped. I was surprised to find that I had a wonderful sense of freedom about the matter, and I didn't feel the need to keep tabs on the social worker. After a couple of weeks had gone by, she phoned me, just to see how I was doing. She, too, was surprised at the peaceful state in which she found me. After years of anxiety, first about infertility, then about adoption, my heart was completely at rest.

When I relinquished the issue of motherhood to God, something happened in my heart—a loosening, a cleansing, a rooting out of something unclean. I was changed, somehow. I became more focused on God, purer. I compare what happened in me to the process that a jeweler might use when refining pure gold. Intense heat melts a lump of metal down to its essential elements. When that happens, the inferior elements—bronze or copper—can be separated. What remains is pure and precious. In that sense, cleansing is a form of loss.

Like a lump of metal, you and I may also be reduced to our essential nature by some crisis, then purified. When God melts us down to the core, exposing the foundation of our thoughts and behavior, it can be painful. But the benefit far outweighs the discomfort, for after God exposes our true nature, he can transform it by removing the attitudes and behaviors that don't belong. Jesus said, "Out of the abundance of the heart the mouth speaks. The good person brings good things out of the good treasure, and the evil person brings evil things out of an evil treasure" (Matt. 12:34–35 NRSV). What's inside of you is who you really are. As the Holy Spirit continues to cleanse your heart, you will lose. You will lose actions or habits that you once held dear; you will lose distance between yourself and God, and between yourself and others. But the you that remains will be purer, freer, better.

That's why it's good to assess your inner core now and then. What are the things that you value most? And what would you do if they were taken away? What would remain in your spirit if you were stripped of every nonessential thing?

In spite of my disappointment, I continued with life pretty much the same as before. I had been cleansed of something—anxiety over my infertility—and that cleansing had created hope within me. I continued to look for God's creative work in my life, but I had no idea what shape that might take. Then, about four weeks after my relinquishment Sunday, Wayne and I received a phone call from some friends in a distant state. They told us of a beautiful baby they thought would be placed for adoption soon, and they offered to find an attorney in their state to pursue the matter for us. We were elated and immediately searched for an attorney in our state to make the connection. On Christmas Eve we received Joella, our beautiful, blond, blue-eyed baby girl.

This was a dream come true! On Christmas day we celebrated with our precious gift. Driving home through the snow and wind, we stopped to eat at a restaurant on the Kansas Turnpike. When we walked in with our darling, wrapped in a pink blanket with matching knit hat, the waitress took one look at her and said, "She's so precious; she looks just like an angel."

If you only knew, I thought. *If you only knew.*

Actually, it was Wayne and I who had no idea what was happening. Without much warning, we had been thrust into the role of parenting. It was awkward at first, learning to change diapers, making formula, juggling the baby's schedule and our own. There were times when I wondered if I could handle it. Then I remembered the relinquishment Sunday, and I knew that I could trust God now as I had then. I continued my job in the inner city, working with people who were on a new track in life also. Some of them were trying to overcome old habits, both in behavior and in thinking. Many times I found myself seeking advice on being a mom from the participants in our program. At times, our roles reversed. I was no longer the omniscient leader with dozens of clients dependent on me. Now, we needed each other; our relationships were reciprocal. In a sense, I lost status. Yet I gained much more. After thirty years, I still maintain friendships with people I met in that program. Blessing is losing, but each loss leads to a gain. Just how much I would gain, however, came as a surprise, even to me.

BLESSING AS LOSS OF FREEDOM

About six months after we brought Joella home, a young woman approached me after church and asked for an appointment with the pastor. She seemed quite upset, but her situation did not appear to be life threatening. Little did I realize that her situation would change *my* life forever.

Seated in Wayne's office, she began tearfully, "A woman I know is going to have a baby. She is going to put her baby up for adoption, and I desperately want to take it. But my husband won't agree." Then she looked directly at me and said, "I think you should take this baby."

My jaw probably touched the floor. *No way,* I thought. *My plate is way too full. Besides, we just adopted a child— six months ago!*

"We'll pray about it," Wayne told her, and we did. We also consulted our lawyer, who reminded us that when having children by adoption, it's best to take them when they are available and not worry about the spacing. He, of course, had a house full of kids and saw "one more" as no problem. He may not have been the most objective advisor in the world, but we took his advice.

On July 31 at 6:00 P.M., the call came with the news: "Congratulations! You are the parents of a baby boy, born today. You may take him home from the hospital in four days." We were elated and scared at the same time. We would soon have two babies, thirteen months apart in age but only seven months apart in our household. We prepared madly for four days, then went to the hospital on a hot August afternoon to greet Eric, our second child. He seemed so tiny. I was sure I wouldn't be able to take care of one so small and fragile. Surely he would break. But my courage grew, and so did he. We survived, somehow, in spite of colic, sleepless nights, oceans of dirty diapers, hundreds of bottles to fill, formula to measure, and schedules to coordinate. Our world had changed overnight, but we couldn't have been happier.

One of the things that we may lose when God blesses us is freedom. Wayne and I lost a good deal of freedom when Joella and Eric arrived so suddenly. Gone were the days when we could determine our own schedules and change plans at a moment's notice. These children were not toys that could be put away and taken out again when it was more convenient. They were a great blessing, but they were also a lifelong responsibility. When God gave us the gift of children, we gave up a measure of freedom. Many of God's blessings exact a toll in the form of responsibility.

Over the years, I have often heard people speak longingly of some "blessing" they wanted to receive. Often, that was a ministry position or career opportunity. Sometimes, when I've heard people bemoan the fact that God has not blessed them with a certain responsibility, I've pressed the issue in conversation. Upon inquiry, it became evident that they had not been responsible in the smaller tasks they'd already been assigned. They wanted the prestige or glory of a greater position but were unwilling to sacrifice the personal freedom that would be required to perform well in it. God's blessings are often disguised as responsibilities— and vice versa. That's true of children, perhaps his greatest earthly gift. It is true as well of marriages, careers, ministries, and even money. We're responsible to manage what God gives us. Generally, people look for shortcuts to the blessings they desire. By doing so, they fail to strengthen their inner core, the base upon which success is built.

BLESSING AS LOSS OF CONTROL

About three years after Eric arrived, we were traveling by car to South Texas to visit relatives. I felt vaguely unwell, but couldn't identify what was wrong. When we got home, I went to the doctor for a checkup. "Maybe you're pregnant," he suggested.

"That can't be it," I said, rapping on the examining room door. "I'm as sterile as this wooden door, remember?"

"Maybe," he said, "but your symptoms suggest that you might be expecting. I think we should check it out."

We did, and I was. Eight months later, John, an eight-and-a-half-pound baby boy joined our family, born from my own body. The impossible had become possible.

The converse was also true, of course. What had once been not merely possible but routine—keeping an orderly household—had now become impossible. The harder I tried, the worse things got. With three children under five years of age, our home seemed in constant chaos. I used to read books on child rearing written by "experts," but I usually wound up questioning their sanity. I wondered, *Why doesn't someone write a book about child rearing when they are surrounded by children?* Then I answered myself immediately: *Because they couldn't. They'd be too busy.*

It occurs to me, however, that that is exactly what Jesus did. He taught us about the kingdom of heaven while living in the midst of human brokenness. He spoke of the value of inner purity in a religious culture that was obsessed only with outward appearances. He taught the value of weakness to a generation that understands only raw power. He patiently taught those who would hear and castigated those who refused to listen.

I buckled down to the task of managing a household of five and soon began to make progress. In time life acquired a semblance of normalcy. That's when I awoke one morning with that same nauseous feeling. *No,* I thought. *It couldn't be. The baby is only six months old. God wouldn't do this to me!*

But he did.

"I guess you've finally reached your childbearing years," the doctor said ironically. "You may have a baby every year." Sure enough, nine months later Mark joined our family. For ten years, it had been just Wayne and I. Now, in less than six years' time, we were a family of six. As we brought child number four into our home, I thought about my relinquishment Sunday, not so very long ago. I wondered what might have happened if I'd chosen the route of resignation? Would I have the wonderful family that I do now?

I really don't know. When I relinquished my infertility to God, I didn't do it in order to get my way. I was simply looking for God's best in my life. Yet I recall the story of Jesus' return visit to Nazareth, his hometown. (See Matt. 13:54–58). When Jesus came home, eager to relieve the suffering of his friends and neighbors, he was rejected. Because the townspeople knew Jesus so well, they couldn't see him as divine, and they wouldn't believe in him. Finally, Jesus left Nazareth, expressing great disappointment. He wanted to do something wonderful for the people, but he couldn't because of their lack of faith. This story haunts me sometimes as I review my own life. Were there times when God would have done more for me—would have given me a greater blessing—if I had been more willing to trust him?

Then I recall that day, sitting on the second row of that inner-city church, when I found the courage to confess my resentment and relinquish my barrenness to God. I believe the result—a family of four wonderful children—is exactly what God wanted for me. At this moment, you may be thinking, *Well, it didn't work for me! I relinquished my infertility to God, and I'm still childless.* You might be thinking a similar thought about a physical disability, a broken relationship, a career crisis, or some other problem in your life. Remember, though, that relinquishing a desire to God does not mean that it will be fulfilled. The essence of relinquishing your situation is to joyfully look forward to what God will do—whatever that may be. I am pleased that God chose to bless me with four children. I believe I would be equally pleased if he had chosen to bless me in some other way instead. When we focus only on our tiny view of the future, we risk missing God's greater vision for our lives.

The journey to complete surrender—relinquishing everything in my life to God—didn't end on that day in church. That was just the beginning. Over the years there have been a number of things I've had to let go of. I once desired a particular job that seemed perfect for me. It was in the right place, working among the right people, and my abilities seemed to match the job description perfectly. But I didn't get the position. What's worse, I thought many things about the hiring process were unfair. This loss, too, had to be relinquished. No, I didn't get a better job later on. In fact, I had to accept a position with less responsibility and less pay. God's vision for my life ultimately led me in a different direction, and I have had to trust him to do what is right. When we "lose" something by relinquishing it to God, we trust him to replace it with something better—

something of his choosing, not ours. Richard Foster says it well: "The Prayer of Relinquishment is a bona fide letting go, but it is a release with hope. We have no fatalist resignation. We are buoyed up by a confident trust in the character of God."[1]

BLESSING AS LOSS OF SELF

Søren Kierkegaard, the nineteenth-century Danish philosopher, was acutely aware of our human tendency to try to manipulate God. In his book *Purity of the Heart Is to Will One Thing,* Kierkegaard says that by constantly relinquishing our lives to God, we come to know him more and more. This knowledge is something more than intellectual. By surrendering ourselves, we become willing to put everything at risk for God. The singleness of motivation results in a deep love for him and for his creation.[2] Kierkegaard expresses that idea in an even stronger way when he writes, "God creates everything out of nothing—and everything which God is to use He first reduces to nothing."[3]

Is it possible that we must lose ourselves completely, that we must become "nothing" in order to find God's blessing? In a very real way, it is. It is only when we surrender ourselves totally—not in one area only—to God, that we may be fully blessed. That doesn't sound good to those of us who have been trained to reach our own potential and develop our self-esteem. But it is only by giving up who we are that we discover who we can be with God's help. God does not want to debase us or cut us down to size; he wants to transform us into something better. Perhaps that experience is best summarized by the Apostle Paul, who said, "I have been crucified with Christ and I no longer live, but Christ lives in me" (Gal. 2:20). After letting go of who he was, he was transformed into the person God wanted him to be.

I had a hard time understanding this principle until one day when I paid a visit to a Toys "R" Us store. Birthdays at our house always meant a trip to Toys "R" Us. This child wonderland was filled with every imaginable type of toy, and choosing a single present was always a dilemma, especially on a family budget. For a couple of years when my boys were younger, it seemed as if we spent hours sorting through the aisle that held the toys knows as Transformers. These fascinating gadgets have folding and retractable parts that could be manipulated to make the toy change from one object into another. A car, for example, might be "transformed" into an outer space hero. It was on one of our birthday excursions, while watching little boys count their money and carefully examine the pictures on the Transformers packages, that I began to see the true meaning of that old and familiar Scripture, Rom. 12:1–2. The Apostle Paul writes, "Do not be conformed to this world, but be transformed by the renewing of your minds, so that you may discern what is the will of God—what is good and acceptable and perfect." As we continually relinquish ourselves to God, he transforms us. With each loss, there is a gain. Following each crucifixion, there is a resurrection. We become a new and different person, shaped by the will of God. What greater blessing could there be?

Theologian Mildred Bangs Wynkoop wrote a small volume on the ministry of the Holy Spirit entitled *Foundations of Wesleyan-Arminian Theology*. There, she makes a statement that has made the power and wonder of the Holy Spirit come alive in my mind. She writes, "The coming of the Holy Spirit means the awakening of the total reserve of human nature. It is a honing of the sharp edge of human energies and capacities in order to fulfill one's God-appointed mission in life."[4] Those words bring hope and energy to my spirit. In them, I see a God who had a vision and place for me in His universe from the very moment of my conception. And as I give to God my desires and dreams, He refines them and shapes them, transforms me into the person that he has intended from the beginning. What confidence! What hope!

TO THINK ABOUT

1. When faced with an insoluble problem, which route are you more likely to choose: resignation or relinquishment?

2. What issue are you facing right now that you may need to relinquish?

3. Do you present yourself to God regularly for cleansing, asking for a pure heart and pure motives?

4. What might need to be removed from your life if you are to receive more from God?

THE BLESSING
OF PURPOSE

*Your calling is the place where your
deep gladness meets the world's deep need.*
—Frederick Buechner

I watched in horror as the images streamed across my television screen. Men and women, stripped of belongings, family members, and dignity, were trudging over mountain passes, fleeing their homes in Kosovo to the safety of Albania. I remember one grandmother who stood before the camera, wailing loudly. "All my family has been killed," she said through a translator, "and I am the only one left." She looked so fragile, so vulnerable. She reminded me of my own grandmother. I began to imagine members of my own family being forced to make that lonely, hopeless journey.

As the battle raged in Kosovo, calls for assistance poured into the office of World Hope International. We soon dispatched both relief teams and resources to Albania to deal with the human crisis as thousands of refugees—ethnic Albanians who had emigrated to Kosovo years earlier—

flooded across the border. The new arrivers quickly filled empty buildings and spilled out into the streets before temporary shelters could be erected. The first challenge for relief workers was simply to keep the people alive.

The situation was aggravated by the tension and prejudice between the incoming refugees and local Albanian people. The Albanians resented their former countrymen, whom they saw as having deserted Albania, now coming back in a time of need. This long-held prejudice made it difficult for many to offer their homes or hands during this crisis. One group, however, displayed a very different attitude—Christians. One relief worker reported: "You won't believe what the new believers are doing here. They work in the buildings all day long, and then at night set up assembly lines to fill bags with food for the people on the streets." Albania's tiny Christian population had overcome their prejudice to extend compassion to those in need.

Albania had been a communist dictatorship for more than fifty years. When the Soviet Union collapsed in the early 1990s, Albania was one of the most isolated countries in the world. In fact, Enver Hoxha, the country's former dictator, was so convinced that the West was going to bomb Albania that he had constructed 700,000 bunkers in this nation of only 3 million people. Not only was Albania isolated from the West, but the teaching of religion was prohibited also. Being caught with a Bible or crucifix would draw an automatic ten-year prison sentence, and the law was readily enforced. During the communist years, there were very few Christians in Albania, and they remained hidden. After the collapse of communism, the door was opened for evangelism, and many responded. Even so, by the time of the war in Kosovo, only about one-tenth of one percent of Albania's population was Christian.

This tiny minority was powerful, though, because it had found a new purpose. These people believed in the power of the gospel. They took literally Jesus' instruction to love and feed one's enemies. As a result this one percent of Albania's population took care of 15 percent of the Kosovar refugees. These Christians were not extraordinary in any other way. They, like most Albanians, had been busy living their own lives, preoccupied with their own survival. Yet when the opportunity to serve came, they responded to the need.

They knew the blessing of purpose.

BLESSING AS PURPOSE

When God blessed Adam and Eve in the Garden of Eden, he gave them a purpose. The Bible says, "God blessed them, and God said to them, 'Be fruitful and multiply, and fill the earth and subdue it; and have dominion over the fish of the sea and over the birds of the air and over every living thing that moves upon the earth'" (Gen. 1:27–28 NRSV). The first human beings were instructed to increase in number and to manage the earth's resources. They were created for a reason.

The Apostle Paul echoes that thought in his writing to the Christians in Ephesus. He says, "For we are God's workmanship, created in Christ Jesus to do good works, which God prepared in advance for us to do" (Eph. 2:8, 9). In other words, our purpose is to do the good things for which we were created. God has something in mind for us. The Albanian Christians had not been culturally conditioned to feed their enemies. They did it because they had the spirit of Christ within them, prompting them to do this good thing.

It is true that nonbelievers often do good things. But remember that at Creation, God blessed his people for his special purpose (Gen. 1:28). Adam and Eve could have carried out their tasks in some one-dimensional way. But they were acting out of God's blessing—the infusion of his character and his presence into them. As believers in Christ, we are heirs to that same blessing. Therefore, when we do good works as people infused with his character, our work takes on another dimension, a spiritual one.

Frank Laubach, father of the literacy movement, is an example of this. Laubach had earned degrees from Princeton University, Union Seminary, and Columbia University when he became a missionary educator in the Philippines in 1915. For ten years he served as dean of education for the University of Manila. In 1925 it was decided to establish a separate administration for the college in Manila, and Laubach desperately wanted the position of college president. Out of courtesy, however, he voted for his opponent and lost the election by one vote.[1]

For several years after that, Laubach battled health problems and despair. He left Manila to take up a new ministry on the island of Mindanao, but because of the conditions on that mission field, Laubach's wife and one surviving child lived nine hundred miles to the north, in Baguio. Behind the cottage where Laubach lived was a place called Signal Hill. Each evening, he would climb to the top with his dog, Tip, seeking companionship with God and hoping to relieve his feelings of loneliness and failure. While walking on Signal Hill on a December evening in 1929, Frank Laubach experienced the defining moment of his life. He described it this way:

> One evening I was sitting on Signal Hill looking over the province that had me beaten. Tip had his nose up under my arm trying to lick the tears off my cheeks. My lips began to move and it seemed to me that God was speaking. "My Child," my lips said, "you have failed because you do not really love these Moros. You feel superior to them because you are white. If you can forget you are an American and think only how I love them, they will respond." I answered back to the sunset, "God, I don't know whether you spoke to me through my lips, but if you did, it was the truth. . . . Drive me out of myself and

102

come and take possession of me and think Thy
thoughts in my mind. . . ."
My lips spoke to me again. "If you want the
Moros to be fair to your religion, be fair to theirs.
Study their Koran with them."[2]

The next day Laubach told some local Muslim leaders he
wanted to study the Koran. They responded enthusiastically.
In a short time, Laubach saw that illiteracy was one of the
greatest problems for the people of Mindinao, and he began
to teach reading. His vision was far greater than one island,
however, and his work gave rise to a worldwide literacy
movement, fueled by prayer. As Laubach put it, "When God
killed my racial prejudice and made me colorblind, it seemed
as though He were working miracles at every turn." It is estimated that some sixty million people have been reached by
his training method, Each One Teach One.

FINDING YOUR PURPOSE

As I studied the life of Frank Laubach, I saw that prayer
was an essential element in his work. Signal Hill was just the
beginning. In his journals, Laubach records many instances
of what he called *flash prayer*. On one occasion he wrote,
"This morning, as I came from the train and prayed for all the
people on the street, I felt a new energy surge into me. What
it does to all of them to receive that instant prayer I may never
know. What it does for me is electrical. It drives out fatigue
and thrills one with eager power."[3] As Laubach prayed, God
blessed him with purpose. The results were far beyond what
he could have achieved based on his own capacity.

LOOK AROUND

When I learned of Laubach's methods, I was eager to
share them with everyone. One day I excitedly related the

idea of sending flash prayers to a group of women at our church. Joybelle responded in a doubtful tone, "That seems a bit far-fetched, but I am going to try it. I take the bus to work every morning, and it's boring. The same people get on every morning with the same complaints. Because I have nothing else to do, I'll send a flash prayer for everyone who gets on the bus and see what happens." I was pleased by this first response, and I hoped that God would "come through" for this new believer.

When we met the next week, Joybelle reported that not much had happened, but sending flash prayers had at least kept her mind off of the complaint-filled conversation that surrounded her each morning. I encouraged her to try the experiment for another week. Would God come through this time?

The next week Joybelle noted that people on the bus were not complaining so much, and people seemed to engage in conversation more. That was not a dramatic start, but Joybelle kept praying. Eventually, she was able to start a daily bus Bible study for commuters traveling from the suburbs to downtown Kansas City, Missouri. The Bible study lasted for several years, and relationships among the riders grew as they began caring for each other even outside the daily commute. Joybelle was not a Bible scholar. In fact, she had many areas of need in her life. But in that daily bus ride, she discovered the blessing of purpose. As she began to listen during the commonplace events of the day, she found God calling to her. The full results of her work may never be known.

HAVE COURAGE

Frank Laubach believed that when a Christian teaches a person to read, the spirit of Jesus is released through the teaching process. That notion parallels the words of Jesus in John 7:38 (NRSV): "Out of the believer's heart shall flow rivers of living water." Another woman in our church group wanted to start a Laubach literacy program as a ministry to the community. Several people thought that would be unnecessary in a middle-class, suburban community. But research showed that there was a significant number of nonreaders in the community, so volunteers were trained in the Laubach method and word was sent out that this service would be available.

Joyce was one of the volunteers. She was eager to teach her first student yet nervous at the same time. Joyce was not a college graduate, but she believed the spirit of Jesus was powerful and that she could succeed in teaching someone to read. Her first student was a cement contractor. The powerfully built man confessed that he could read blueprints but was dependent on his wife to do all the book work for his business. He tried to cover up his illiteracy, but as his children grew, they began to wonder why he would not help them with homework. Joyce began to teach, and before long, the cement contractor was reading the newspaper.

MOVE BEYOND

Joybelle and Joyce found their purpose in the course of their everyday lives. Joybelle worked for an insurance company, and Joyce was a homemaker with a husband and three sons. For some others, finding God's purpose may require getting away from the routine and into another environment. I have known many people who embarked on a mission trip thinking they were going to greatly affect the lives of the people to whom they would minister. Often, these "givers" find that they are the ones who receive ministry, and their own lives are changed as a result. Some have made decisions either to serve full-time overseas or to regularly give the gift of time or money to the people of another culture.

Sometimes finding purpose takes one in a completely different direction, one that may require a demotion—at least in the eyes of others. I have a friend who held a position of authority in a corporation. He was highly respected, managed large budgets, and wrote books that brought about change in the corporate culture. Yet deep within, he longed to teach at a university where he could be a mentor to young people, shaping the faith and values of those who would change the world. When he resigned his executive position in order to teach, his colleagues were stunned. But his inner core was strong, and he had the courage to find and follow his purpose. Today there are many graduates whose lives have been shaped by the influence of this brave leader.

One's purpose may change in different phases of life. There may come a point where old passions do not burn as hot. To continue would best serve neither the individual nor others. I have found that during those times, life seems empty; it appears to be an endless routine with little meaning. Yet change is intimidating and uncertain. How do you know if it is time for change? How do you gather the courage to change? In the same way as you originally found your purpose: by listening to God.

Frederick Buechner offers this insight: "Listen to your life. See it for the fathomless mystery it is. In the boredom and pain of it no less than in the excitement and gladness: touch, taste, smell your way to the holy and hidden heart of it because in the last analysis all moments are key moments, and life itself is grace."[4]

PURSUING YOUR PURPOSE

Frank Laubach's literacy work took him to nearly every continent in the world. He met with kings, prime ministers, presidents, and generals. That literacy movement continues today. Perhaps Laubach's own words best sum up the relationship between blessing and purpose. He said, "God, what is man's best gift to mankind? To be beautiful of soul and then let people see into your soul."[5]

The nameless Albanian believers who tirelessly served the Kosovar refugees were unknowingly beautiful of soul.

Their loving efforts allowed the leaders of their nation to see the beauty of Christ. As a result, I had the privilege to be invited along with other Christian leaders to meet with the president, prime minister, and supreme court justices of Albania to discuss the rebuilding of their country.

As I sat at dinner that evening in the home of President Rexhep Meidani and his wife, I couldn't help but think of the hours, the love, the care and the endless days and nights that those Christians, a tiny minority in their country, had given to assisting the refugees. Little did these believers know the effect they had on the future of their country. As the conversation deepened, President Meidani asked a penetrating question: "How can I build a moral fiber in this country?" He went on to explain that he was neither a Christian nor a Communist but a secularist. In spite of that, he believed that a nation needs moral fiber to survive. Many ideas were posed and discussed. Having an academic background President Meidani realized the importance not only of education but also of the philosophy behind it. Again our attention was arrested when he asked, "Is it possible to start a Christian university here in this country?" As we said good-bye that evening, I thought how different things might be if the Albanian Christians, just 0.1 percent of their country's population, had not pursued the purpose with which God had blessed them.

We've seen that Adam and Eve were made in God's image as social beings and that both of them were given dominion over creation (Gen. 1:26–28). Both were told to fill the earth and subdue it and to be fruitful and multiply. Theologians sometimes refer to these commands as *cultural mandates*. God was saying to Adam and Eve, in effect, "I have given you intelligence, and I have blessed you with my character and power. I have opened the world and all its possibilities to you; therefore, go and be active in it." Both Adam and Eve are leaders with authority.

God is telling us these same things today. Every aspect of our world—politics, science, medicine, law, education, theology, business, art, music, and every other—belongs to the people of God. God does not make a distinction between Christian pursuits and worldly pursuits. He is present in all disciplines. It is the manner in which we pursue them that makes them Christian.

Yet pursuing your purpose will not be simple. Along the way you are sure to face problems and choices that may discourage you from seizing opportunities. Here are some things to be aware of as you act on the purpose God has set before you.

CONSERVATION

Adam and Eve's first order of business was to care for and preserve the creation in a way that reflects the loving ordered relationship between creation and God himself. That mandate has not expired. We, like Adam and Eve, are commissioned to preserve the earth, not to consume it. Therefore, no understanding of our purpose can be complete without considering where we fit into the whole of God's creation.

It is disheartening that the people of God have by and large neglected the call to care for the creation; it is secularists who have taken the lead in this area. My own environmental convictions have grown over the years. In March 1999 I chaired a conference with the theme "Compassion and the Care of Creation," sponsored by the National Association of Evangelicals and the Evangelical Environmental Network. Thoughtful papers were presented followed by challenging responses. One presenter, Professor Stephan Bouma-Prediger of Hope College in Holland, Michigan, made this bold statement:

> We are to fulfill our calling to be earthkeepers, regardless of whether global warming is real or there are holes in the ozone layer or three nonhuman species a day are going extinct. Our vocation as caretakers of creation is not contingent on results or on the state of the earth. It is, simply,

dependent on our calling and character as God's responsible human image-bearers."[6]

Discipleship is the foundation for Christian environmentalism. It is not a cause to be advocated but divine purpose, one given to us at Creation. As we pursue our purpose, we must be mindful of how we are using God's world and the resources in it.

CALLING

The term *vocation* has lost most of its power in our culture. Essentially, we think of a vocation as any job, not necessarily even a profession. A vocational school is a trade school. A vocation is anything one does for a living.

Originally, the term meant something more. A vocation was a calling, a task given to one by God. The Puritans used the two terms—*vocation* and *calling*—interchangeably. They saw that work done with the hands or the mind can be a sacred thing, a channel of divine love. Elton Trueblood, a Quaker theologian and philosopher, said, "We should see the ordination to the priesthood as a sacrament; but we should likewise see ordination to any worthwhile human task as a sacrament."[7]

My sister, Shirley, was gifted with an incredible singing voice and began singing in church at a very young age. Then in junior high school, Shirley heard an opera for the first time. She was hooked. Because our church discouraged attendance at the theater, no one in our family had ever been to an opera. That was a truly foreign world to us, and seemed to be something a Christian should not pursue. In college, Shirley studied music and voice and was encouraged to pursue opera. But my parents, being the practical people they were, suggested she prepare herself for a "real job." I'm sure they also thought that the opera house was no place for their highly talented daughter. How could God use her gift in the theater?

Equipped with a music education degree, my sister made her way west to California and taught music in a junior high school in the Los Angeles public school system. A few months into the school year, Shirley realized neither she nor the students thought she was in the right profession. The next fall, she entered graduate school at the University of Southern California, where she earned a master's degree in voice performance. There, Shirley began to sense her purpose. She felt God's blessing as she sang, and began to see that opera was her "calling." The experiences she has had singing in opera houses all over the world would fill a book, one which I will let her write. Suffice it to say that her story is replete with instances of God's guidance, discipline, and blessing. She found her calling and God's blessing in it.

COURAGE

To pursue your purpose takes courage. Even if you have a clear direction and God's blessing, you may be fearful of taking the first step. Joshua, one of the greatest leaders in the Bible, must have had that problem, because God repeatedly had to tell him to be courageous. The old rabbis used to say that the Red Sea did not part for the children of Israel until the water got to their nostrils. I can certainly identify with that. There have been many times I felt as if I were about to drown when the waters finally parted.

Philippe Vernier, a leader in the field of prayer and meditation, speaks eloquently of the need to pursue your purpose courageously. He writes:

> Therefore do not wait for great strength before setting out, for immobility will weaken you further. Do not wait to see very clearly before starting: one has to walk toward the light. Have you strength enough to take this first step? Courage enough to accomplish this little tiny act of fidelity or reparation, the necessity of which is apparent to you? Take this step! Perform this act! You will be astonished to feel that the effort accomplished, instead of having

exhausted your strength, has doubled it, and that you already see more clearly what you have to do next.[8]

CONFLICT

In whatever endeavor you are involved, you will face conflicts. Often, those conflicts will be between you and another person. It is always a struggle to know when to confront another person about an issue and when to allow time for the problem to resolve itself. There is a time and place for both methods, and neither is easy. Learning to manage conflict is part of learning to manage creation, the task that God has assigned to us. Conflict management is a science of its own, and there are dozens of books on the subject. Yet at a minimum, you must realize that you will face conflict. Don't be surprised when it happens. Some of us—I include myself—tend to take the naïve view that if everything is as it should be, there will be no conflict. That's nonsense, of course. The pursuit of your purpose will inevitably bring you into contact with people who have different goals. Even if you are working toward the same end, you won't always agree on how to get there.

Those who aren't prepared for conflict tend to view themselves as martyrs when conflict occurs. "Well," they decide, "this must all be my fault. So I guess I'll just walk away." Withdrawal is a form of passive manipulation that is often learned in childhood. Although an unhealthy way of dealing with conflict, it is at least familiar. Recently, I faced a series of conflicts and was embarrassed to find myself falling back into that childish model. *I'll just quit,* I thought. *Then they'll be sorry and agree to see things my way.* There were no thunderbolts from heaven, but I did have a keen sense of humiliation when I realized that I was being immature. How much better it is to be courageous, to face difficult issues unemotionally, sorting out the various motives and possibilities to arrive at what's best for everyone involved. The ability to do that is important for pursuing purpose.

111

CHANGE

A final challenge in pursuing purpose is to maintain a fresh focus on your calling. That's especially hard to do when working with a group of people. Purpose-driven groups generally begin with a clear goal and lots of energy, but they tend to go flat over time. They become less vigorous, less effective, and even less certain about what they are doing. They may continue to be active but have no clear idea of their purpose.

That was the case in 1990 when a group of women leaders in our church sat around a conference table trying to determine what to do in the next year. We knew that we could do the same old things—have a Bible study here and there, organize a few outings, do some fundraising—but it seemed that God was stirring our hearts to accomplish something more. But what? We left that night with a few tentative ideas on the drawing board and a plan to meet again in a few weeks. Sometime before the next meeting, the state director of Prison Fellowship Ministries phoned me to ask if I knew of any women who might volunteer to minister at Renz Correctional Facility, a maximum security women's prison near Jefferson City, Missouri, about ninety miles from our community. She went on to say that the prison's population was increasing rapidly, and there was no ministry being offered there. Existing ministries had all been designed for men, and Prison Fellowship ministries leaders were struggling to create programs to serve the female prisoners.

I invited the director to attend the next meeting of our women's group, and she suggested bringing the prison superintendent along to talk with our women. I agreed reluctantly, for I certainly wasn't energized by this opportunity. The logistics seemed overwhelming, and I didn't think our women, most of whom worked full-time jobs, would be eager to drive that distance and try to make a significant connection with, well, criminals. Also, in the back of my mind was this nagging thought: *We're supposed to be building our own church, here in Warrenton. Those inmates certainly won't help us do that. They'll never volunteer time or donate money—they can't even attend church!*

When our meeting began, all of the women in our group were skeptical. But as the discussion continued, we felt the presence of the Holy Spirit. Finally, we agreed to help and arrived at a plan, one that I would never have chosen.

"Let's use the prison gymnasium," one woman suggested. "We can invite all the women from the prison, have a speaker and some music, and maybe do something fun. We can set up tables, and each of us can be a table hostess. We'll serve dessert following the program and offer door prizes."

The other women agreed enthusiastically. "We can give them a feeling of hope and dignity," one said. "And if they want to know more about Jesus, we'll invite them to the Prison Fellowship Bible study."

My training in sociology told me that this plan was completely laughable. We were going to do this middle-class ladies' tea with some of the roughest criminals in the state. But I didn't have a better idea, so I agreed.

It was a sunny fall day when twenty-five women from our church carpooled to the maximum security prison for women at Renz. We were fearful. Only one or two had ever been inside a prison. I had visited only a small county jail. We knew that we were in over our heads. Having recently read about a prison riot and the lack of adequate prison staff in our state didn't help my confidence level any.

When we arrived, both the prison superintendent and the state director of Prison Fellowship met us at the gate. Their presence began to allay my fears. Soon we began to unload our vehicles and set up for the event. After a few minutes, I noticed that there were some inmates helping us. I was surprised by their appearance. They looked so . . . normal. Frankly, they looked just like the women in our church group. I knew these women weren't in prison because they'd had a parking ticket. They had committed serious, even violent, crimes. Yet I began to see that they were very much like us.

A few minutes later, the guards opened the doors and three hundred women came through the steel portals into the gym. My blood pressure increased a little when I realized there were only four guards present. Then I glanced around at the tables, and tears came to my eyes. Seated nearby was one of the genuine saints of our church, a beautiful older woman, wearing a simple but elegant gray suit with pink blouse, her gray hair perfectly coifed, and a serene smile upon her face. Verneda was engaged in a conversation with one of the prisoners, a tough looking woman who sported tattoos on both arms, smoked profusely, and carried herself with a masculine bearing. *This is the kingdom of God,* I thought, *God's grace for all.*

We proceeded with our program, and at the end of the session, I drew names for door prizes. I loudly read either the name or the identification number, whichever the person chose to use. The fourth name I read caused my blood to run cold. I recognized the name of this woman, who had been convicted in a highly visible case. She and her husband had been simple farmers, but they devised a plan to murder transient people, bury them on their farm, then collect the victims' Social Security benefits. This woman, Faye Copeland, and her husband were both sentenced to death. I stumbled while reading the name, barely able to spit out the words. Faye stepped forward. Her gray hair was parted severely down the middle and hung limply around her face. I looked straight into this elderly woman's eyes and thought how empty they looked. *This is a woman without a soul,* I couldn't help myself from thinking.

Faye's face haunted me for the next month. Emma Lee, the woman from our church who had been her hostess, made her a prayer project, so I heard Faye's name every week. The next month when we returned to Renz, Emma Lee invited Faye to sit with her again. I noticed that even more women had attended this month. We were all more relaxed, and the day was fantastic. When it came time for the door prizes, I was astonished when, out of some three hundred names, I again drew Faye's name. I braced myself as she stepped forward to receive her prize. I was shocked, but this time at the change. Faye looked ten years younger, and there was something different about her. She had life in her eyes. As soon as the event was over, I made my way to Janice Webb, the state director for Prison Fellowship. "What in the world has happened to Faye?" I asked.

"I have been so eager to tell you," she said. "Faye came to your meeting the last time because she heard there might be food, but then she became interested in learning more about Jesus. She came to the Prison Fellowship Bible study that week, and there she prayed for Jesus to forgive her, cleanse her heart, and fill her with his presence."

While the director was still talking, Emma Lee rushed over and said, "I have got to tell you what Faye said when she was telling me of her new faith. She said, 'Isn't it interesting I had to come to prison to find my freedom?'" We all stood there speechless, tears flowing down our cheeks.

Each time we returned, Faye brought more women to our meetings. Some of them also had been convicted of highly visible crimes. I thought I recognized one of the women, so I asked the director about her. Sure enough, she was the culprit in a high profile case I'd read about.

"But she's a Muslim," I said. "I'm surprised she's here."

"She's a Christian now," the director replied. "Faye brought her to the Lord."

Faye began to reach out in other ways as well. She sought permission to beautify the prison compound by planting flowers. Other prisoners joined her, many of whom had never planted a flower in their lives. Faye taught them gardening, sewing, quilting, and other crafts.

Faye Copeland held the record for the oldest woman on death row. Her picture appeared in *Time* and *Newsweek* magazines during some death row debates. She outlived her husband who died in prison of natural causes. In 1999 her death sentence was overturned, and in 2002, twelve years after my first encounter with her, Faye was paroled due to health reasons. She was released from prison to live in a nursing home.

Nameless Albanian Christians find the courage to change the course of a nation. A brokenhearted educator starts a worldwide movement that teaches tens of thousands to read. A frightened, middle-class lady and a hopeless death row inmate together discover the blessing of new life.

That is the power of purpose. That is the blessing that God has for you.

TO THINK ABOUT

1. What is your greatest desire?

2. Describe a time when you believe God was prompting you to accomplish some task.

3. What do you think God wants you to do now?

4. What factors might make it difficult to pursue your purpose? Name some ways that you might deal with those factors?

THE BLESSING
OF SUFFERING

*He who has a why to live for can
bear with almost any how.*
—Friedrich Nietzsche

H e stood there in the doorway saying good-bye, his
shoulders stooped, skin leather-like from years in
the Indian sun, eyes dim and moist. We were leaving
Gujarat, India, to return to the United States. Dr. Samuel
Justin, an Indian pastor and leader, would remain to carry
on the fight.

"Continue to pray for us," he said tearfully. "The persecution is great, but it seems the more the persecution, the
more God blesses." As the plane lifted off the ground, I knew
I might never see this brave friend again.

It seems odd to speak of God's blessing in persecution,
yet Samuel Justin had grasped the truth of this paradox. A
radical Hindu sect had placed a death sentence on this gentle
Christian pastor. Although Samuel is always respectful of
Hindus and careful not to offend them, they find him a danger.

Why? It is because he embodies the love of Jesus Christ, and as a result, many Hindus have converted to Christianity.

When local authorities heard that the radical sect had placed a price on Samuel's head, they determined to protect him. Officers of the Indian secret police were assigned to keep him under their surveillance. The added security did not slow Samuel down, however, and continued his work by teaching, preaching, starting schools, caring for the sick, and simply loving people.

I was privileged to be in Pardee, India, on a Sunday morning when nearly one thousand people had gathered for worship and a baptismal service. Samuel Justin invited me to assist in the baptism and informed me that among the candidates were two members of the Indian secret police. "They were Hindus," Samuel said, "but they converted to Christianity."

"How did you meet these men?" I asked. Samuel just smiled in reply. Then it dawned on me that these were the secret police who had literally been watching Samuel. During their surveillance, they had been drawn to Christ by his example. These men were so affected by his silent witness that they chose to leave the security of their ancestral religion and risk their lives by publicly declaring their allegiance to Jesus Christ. As I baptized these brave men and their wives, I couldn't help but wonder whether anyone who happened to follow me around would be so impressed by my life that they would choose to follow Jesus.

BLESSING AS PERSECUTION

It was Jesus who made the connection between blessing and persecution explicit. In his Sermon on the Mount, he said, "Blessed are you when people insult you, persecute you and falsely say all kinds of evil against you because of me. Rejoice and be glad, because great is your reward in heaven, for in the same way they persecuted the prophets who were before you" (Matt. 5:11–12). Jesus knew that there is a depth of peace in persecution that only those who share it can realize. The Apostle Paul knew this when he spoke of the "fellowship of sharing in [Christ's] suffering" (Phil. 3:10). The Apostle Peter also referred to the blessing of suffering on many occasions.

The backdrop to these writings has always intrigued me. For much of the first century, the Roman government made no distinction between Christians and Jews. Christianity was considered a Jewish sect, and was therefore a *religio licita*, or legal religion. That changed in A.D. 64.

PERSECUTION IN THE EARLY CHURCH

Nero was emperor of Rome when a great fire broke out in the city in A.D. 64. The blaze spread through the narrow streets, consuming homes, businesses, shrines, and temples. For days the fire raged, sometimes appearing to be under control, then breaking out in other parts of the city. Nero watched the fire from a safe distance and said that he was "charmed with the flower and loveliness of the flames."[1]

After the fire, the Roman people were irate and bitter, and they blamed Nero for the inferno. Taking advice from Aliturus, his favorite actor and Poppaea, his mistress, Nero accused the little-known Christian sect of setting the blaze.[2] Brutal persecution of Christians soon followed. Nero led the way, ordering unbelievable acts of cruelty against believers. Some Christians were covered in pitch, then set afire as living torches for Nero's garden parties. He ordered that others be sewn into the skins of wild animals, then hunted by dogs. Many believers were crucified or burned to death.[3] Christianity no longer enjoyed the quiet anonymity of a Jewish sect. Christianity had become an unlawful religion, it's members subject to the confiscation of their property and brutal violence.

Since there was no worldwide cable news network at the time, word of the persecution in Rome spread by letter. Peter wrote to warn Christians about it (1 Pet. 5:8). Believers never knew when persecution might break out in their town, and roving mobs would unexpectedly enter a city in search of Christians. Many local governors were willing to believe the slander that was being spread about Christians and welcomed those who would root them out. Persecution, like the fire of Rome, would come under control in one place only to break out again somewhere else. Christians lived in terror for many years.

PERSECUTION IN SCRIPTURE

In spite of the persecution that they suffered, Peter believed that Christians were blessed. He wrote, "If you are insulted because of the name of Christ, you are blessed, for the Spirit of glory and of God rests on you" (1 Pet. 4:14). Later in the same letter, he wrote, "If you should suffer for what is right, you are blessed" (3:14). Peter went on to list what he saw as four benefits of persecution: it would restore Christians and make them strong, firm, and steadfast (5:10).

The Greek word translated *restore* means to supply what is missing or mend what is broken. Suffering, then, if accepted in trust and love, can mend the weakness in a person's character and build up faith. The Greek word translated *strong* comes from the word for granite. The word translated *firm* carries the idea of being filled with strength. *Steadfast* refers to the laying of a foundation. Suffering and persecution strip away every useless thing from our lives. Then, only what is steadfast, firm, and strong remains. That's why suffering builds faith. It forces us to rely on the one thing that is truly reliable—God. Incredible as it seems, suffering adds grace to our lives.

THE EXAMPLE OF PERPETUA

I never cease to be amazed at the power of God manifested in the lives of first-generation Christians, both now and in the early church. One of the earliest records of persecution comes to us from a young woman named Perpetua. Born in A.D. 180, Perpetua was from a distinguished family in Carthage, the leading city in North Africa. At a young age, she heard the gospel and could not resist the claims of Christ. In 202, Perpetua was accused of being a Christian and was placed in a common prison with twelve others. She writes, "I was terrified, as I had never before been in such a dark hole. What a difficult time it was." Perpetua was a nursing mother and also felt the added anxiety of being separated from her son. Her father visited her in prison and begged her to renounce her faith. "Have pity on your father's gray head," he begged. "Have pity on your infant son. Offer the sacrifice for the welfare of the emperors."

"I will not," Perpetua replied adamantly.

Perpetua was condemned to die in the Roman amphitheater in Carthage, and her death was a slow one. First, she was stripped naked and placed in a net where she was tossed into the air by mad heifers. She said to those around her, "You must all stand fast in the faith and love one another, and do not be weakened by what we have gone through." Perpetua survived that ordeal, which meant that she would be put to death by the sword. The gladiator assigned to slay her nervously took aim and slipped as he thrust his sword. Perpetua was injured, but the wound was not fatal. She emitted a brief scream, then she took the trembling hand of the young gladiator and guided the blade to her throat.[4]

Perpetua was one of thousands who discovered that the presence of God is real even in persecution. We are blessed even when we suffer.

FINDING FAITH IN SUFFERING

We often blur the distinction between persecution and suffering, probably because we North American Christians are not persecuted. Persecution is suffering, but suffering is not necessarily persecution. Rejection, while not as violent or cruel as persecution, is also a source of suffering. Many who are not overtly persecuted experience some form of social rejection because of their faith, and that produces very real suffering.

I've known some folk who have experienced a painful combination of suffering and rejection. Debilitated by some dreaded illness, they have exhausted every possibility for healing and continue to live in pain. Added to their discomfort are the harsh remarks of other Christians who believe that the continued illness indicates a lack of faith.

While not strictly the same, persecution and suffering are similar in that they both produce greater dependence upon God; therefore, many of the lessons from persecution can be applied to those who suffer. As Scripture so often reminds us, there is blessing in suffering.

But where? And how does one find it?

KEEPING FAITH

Admiral Jim Stockdale was the highest ranking American officer to be held prisoner of war in Vietnam. He was confined from 1965 to 1973 in the infamous North Vietnamese prison known as the "Hanoi Hilton." There he was tortured more than twenty times, had no prisoner's rights, and no set release date. He, like every POW, was uncertain when or if he would ever go home.

In the book *In Love and War,* Stockdale describes how he tried to maintain the emotional strength of his fellow prisoners so that they could both survive and resist the enemy's attempts to use them for propaganda. He taught the men to communicate by tapping out letters in a simple code. One day the prisoners who were sweeping and mopping the prison's central yard tapped out the words "we love you" to Stockdale.[5]

Author and researcher Jim Collins spent an afternoon with Stockdale on the campus of Stanford University where he asked the retired admiral how he and other prisoners coped with the uncertainty of their situation. Stockdale replied, "I never lost faith in the end of the story. I never doubted not only that I would get out, but also that I would prevail in the end and turn the experience into the defining event of my life, which, in retrospect, I would not trade."[6] Incredibly, even in captivity, Stockdale understood that his suffering was somehow a form of blessing.

Collins then asked, "Who didn't make it out?"

"Oh, that's easy," responded Stockdale, "the optimists." Then the admiral explained his remark. "The optimists . . . were the ones who said, 'We're going to be out by Easter.' And Easter would come, and Easter would go. And then Thanksgiving, and then it would be Christmas again. And they died of a broken heart." After a long pause, Stockdale said, "This is a very important lesson. You must never confuse faith that you will prevail in the end—which you can never afford to lose—with the discipline to confront the most brutal facts of your current reality, whatever they might be."[7] Faith is not naïve optimism. It is the belief that God will prevail in every situation. Stockdale survived because he kept the faith.

CONFRONTING REALITY

Confronting the "brutal facts" of reality moves us out of the realm of martyrs and heroes and into daily life. Not everyone will face some tragically heroic death in the arena, but all of us must face the relentless grind of day-to-day living. Those daily experiences can add up to a sort of low-grade, continual suffering. Your own brutal facts might include the following:

- Working on the assembly line of an automobile plant, doing the same twist of bolts and screws hundreds of times a day while listening to the cursing, complaining, and boring banter of those around you.

- Realizing at midlife that the dreams you had for your professional life will never be realized.
- Looking into the eyes of teenage children and praying that they will not continue on the path of bad choices they have begun.
- Struggling with doubts about the existence of God and wondering what happened to the firm convictions that you once felt.
- Being pastor to people who have unrealistic expectations and dealing with agonizing, inward self-doubt.

Oddly, blessing is found in confronting the very situations that seem to be causes of suffering. When we express our situation honestly to God in prayer, giving a name to the brutal reality, we find God's presence and peace. Peter is on target again when he writes, "Therefore, let those suffering in accordance with God's will entrust themselves to a faithful Creator, while continuing to do good" (1 Pet. 4:19).

SEEKING GOD

It's tempting to spiritualize people who have been persecuted for the faith. We do that when we believe they have never doubted God or never confronted him with the brutal facts of their situation. By doing so, we place those Christians in a different category than ourselves, who experience more mundane forms of suffering. In fact, we tend to discount our low-grade suffering as not valued by God. But God may be found in all suffering, both great and small.

Kimpo was a bright young university graduate in Myanmar and an enthusiastic follower of Jesus. In early 2000 Kimpo was invited to attend a conference for itinerant evangelists in Amsterdam, Holland, sponsored by the Billy Graham Evangelistic Association. He was thrilled beyond belief to have received such an invitation and went immediately to apply for a visa. At the government office, Kimpo presented the required documentation to an official who eyed him warily. The official left the room and returned a few minutes later with two officers. They arrested Kimpo, placed him in shackles, and led him to prison.

Myanmar is a country not friendly to Christians. Irish rock star Bono, of the band U2, has even taken note of the country, sharply criticizing its regime in a song. One of Myanmar's own citizens, Daw Aung San Suu Kyi, leader of the National League for Democracy, received the Nobel Peace Prize for her pro-democracy writings but was unable to travel to Oslo, Norway, to accept it because she was under house arrest.

Given the situation in Myanmar, Kimpo was not surprised at being arrested. He had been publicly proclaiming his faith, and he knew that persecution was possible. Even so, he couldn't help but be confused and fearful. Would this be the end of his work as an evangelist? Would this be the end of his life?

The young evangelist was allowed to have visitors on the weekends, and his friends came regularly. They assured Kimpo that they were praying for him and felt sure that God would arrange some miraculous release, as he'd done for Peter in the New Testament. Yet the weeks went by and nothing changed. Desperately, Kimpo's friends gathered even more people to fast and pray for his release. Kimpo himself became convinced that he would soon be free.

Things grew only worse, however. The isolation that he felt and the silence from prison officials became almost unbearable. Finally, Kimpo cried out to God: "Have you forgotten about me? Nothing seems to be happening. I have been a wonderful evangelist for you here in Myanmar. This is a very tough country. You should be happy with what I have done!" Kimpo later told me that he felt guilty about that prayer, but the words expressed his true feelings at the time. When he gave voice to those thoughts, Kimpo began to face the brutal facts of his situation.

The next day a prisoner came to Kimpo and said, "I have been watching you. You keep reading that book all the time.

What is it?" Kimpo explained that it was the Bible. The prisoner began to ask more questions, which allowed the intrepid evangelist to share the gospel. Finally, the man had the courage to pray with Kimpo and become a follower of Jesus. A similar event took place the next day and the day after that. When his friends arrived that weekend, Kimpo shocked them with a request. "Tell all the people praying for my release to change their prayers," he said. "Tell them to pray that I stay here in prison. God has a task for me to do." His friends were dumbfounded. They had never thought of imprisonment in those terms. "I do have one other request," Kimpo added. "Please gather Bibles and discipleship materials for me to use here."

As the months passed, Kimpo led 233 prisoners to faith in Jesus Christ. Then one day a guard appeared at the door of the evangelist's cell. "Get up," he commanded. "You're being moved to another ward." Kimpo was placed in an isolated ward with twenty of the worst criminals in Myanmar. There he was shackled, with a bar placed between his legs so that he could barely move around. Yet even there, seven of the twenty fellow prisoners found hope for their future in Jesus Christ. After several weeks a guard appeared at Kimpo's cell and told him he was free to go.

I was with Kimpo just three weeks after his release. He moved slowly because his muscles had atrophied in prison. Yet there was a fire in his heart and hope in his spirit. As he relayed this story to me, he concluded with tears in his eyes, "I was in prison for eight months and never made it to the Billy Graham conference. But God had a greater conference for me to attend." He went on to tell of his vision for the orphan children in the homes he was supervising. "I intend for these children to have the best education, health, and care," he said doggedly. "I am training them all to be evangelists in Myanmar."

I observed Kimpo as he related both to the children under his care and to us foreign visitors. The mysterious, joyous, gracious presence of Christ surrounded him. In that brave young man, I saw what Peter meant when he said, "If you are reviled for the name of Christ, you are blessed, because the spirit of glory, which is the Spirit of God is resting on you"(1. Pet. 4:14). I don't think Kimpo would have arrived at that place of peace if he had not sought God honestly, ruthlessly confronting the reality of his situation and laying bare his soul before the Lord. By doing so, he was able to move beyond wistful, plastic optimism to genuine faith.

FINDING HOPE IN SUFFERING

While not the same as persecution, suffering is similar to it in that both experiences drive us to a greater dependence upon God. That means that the lessons from persecution may be applied to those who suffer. In either case, we live in hope.

HOPE AS PURPOSE

Viktor Frankl was a prisoner in the concentration camps of Auschwitz and Dachau during World War II. There the Austrian psychiatrist learned the powerful lesson of hope, which he relates in the book *Man's Search for Meaning,* a volume that has influenced an entire generation both personally and in the field of psychotherapy. Frankl states that "any attempt to restore a man's inner strength in the camp had first to succeed in showing him some future goal."[8] That future goal, however, could not be external. It had to be something within the prisoner.

Frankl tells of his senior block warder, a composer, who confided one day, "I have had a strange dream. A voice told me that I could wish for something, that should only say what I wanted to know, and all my questions would be answered. What do you think I asked? That I would like to know when the war would be over for me. You know what I mean, Doctor—for me! I wanted to know when we, when our camp, would be liberated and our sufferings come to an end."

Frankl inquired as to when he had had this dream. The man said that it was in February. The man then whispered that the camp would be liberated on March 30. It was now early March, and the composer was filled with expectation and energy. But March 30 came, and the camp was not liberated. The war was not over; there was no deliverance. Almost immediately, the composer became delirious, then lost consciousness altogether. On March 31, he was dead. The cause of death was given as typhus, but Frankl believed otherwise. He wrote, "The ultimate cause of my friend's death was that the expected liberation did not come and he was severely disappointed. This suddenly lowered his body's resistance against the latent typhus infection. His faith in the future and his will to live had become paralyzed and his body fell victim to illness—and thus the voice in his dream was right after all."[9]

Frankl noted a parallel between the composer's experience and the camp's death rate for the week between Christmas 1944 and New Year's Day 1945. It was higher than in previous years, and the explanation did not lie in food supplies, change of weather, or harder working conditions. The difference was that the prisoners had lived in the naïve hope that they would be home again by Christmas. When that did not happen, they lost hope, and their resistance to disease decreased. Frankl concludes: "We began to discover that it did not really matter what we expected from life, but rather what life expected from us."[10]

Frankl's conclusion resembles Friedrich Nietzsche's comment that "he who has a *why* to live for can bear with almost any *how*." I believe Peter gets at the "why" of life in 1 Pet. 4:13, where he speaks of "sharing Christ's sufferings." When we live for Christ, identifying with him so completely that we desire to share even in his suffering, we move beyond the artificial limits of time and date and into the realm of hope.

HOPE AS POWER

It's unlikely that we will be interred in a concentration camp, as Victor Frankl was. Yet the principle of hope applies to our low-grade suffering just as it did to the greater suffering there. We are blessed when we suffer because we experience the power of hope, which builds our inner core, enabling us to better reflect God's glory. That is not to say that we seek suffering. Yet I have seen families drawn together and lives enriched even in the midst of painful suffering, such as the illness and death of a loved one.

I knew one young friend who as a prisoner not in a concentration camp but in her own, debilitated body. She suffered constant pain as her health slowly deteriorated. Yet she stubbornly resisted her disease, insisting on hiking with her husband, capably caring for her two young children, and traveling overseas. She prays for healing, but believes as Frankl does that life expects something of her. She continues to fight her disease—continues to be alive—because she has hope. It is hope that invigorates her and gives her the determination to keep going. She has a "why," a reason to live.

HOPE AS DETERMINATION

We generally think of suffering as a physical experience; it can be emotional as well. And suffering can have many causes, including finances. Many people have taken their own lives following a severe financial loss. Fearing the embarrassment and difficult changes that would follow, they succumbed to despair, the opposite of hope.

I once spoke at a retreat along with a man who appeared to be very wealthy. After he shared his story, I had a new understanding of the suffering that financial loss can bring. This man, whom I'll call Ron Jefferson, had designed a helmet that was used by the military. He ran a very successful business and was awarded several contracts to produce the helmet for the armed forces. Money seemed to be rolling in, and the Jeffersons were very generous; they contributed liberally to churches, colleges, mission boards, and other worthwhile organizations. They had a constant stream of social invitations from church officials and civic leaders.

Then things changed. The defense contracts dried up, and Ron made some bad business decisions. As a result, the Jeffersons were forced to sell their large home, big cars, jewels, and everything else that had significant worth. Suddenly, the church seemed less interested in Ron. Rejection by his Christian friends hurt him even more than the financial loss.

The couple owned a small piece of land on the outskirts of town. "So," Ron said, "we bought a cheap trailer and pulled it out on that property. We began to attend a small church where people loved us in spite of the fact that we had nothing."

Things were still difficult, however. The wind would blow so hard at times that Ron feared the trailer might blow over. "My wife kept begging me to put a metal skirt around the trailer to keep the wind out, but I wouldn't," Ron said. "That would mean we've given up," he told her. "But I'm not planning to stay here." The family caught the spirit of hope in Ron's words. They worked together to revive the business, and it was eventually restored. "More important than the financial success," Ron said, "was the closeness of our family and the presence of God during those days." The blessing of suffering a financial loss brought them to a new dependence on God and a real experience of hope.

I had always loved the word *hope,* but the idea behind it was elusive to me. What is hope? How would you describe it? Finally I hit upon an analogy that helps me understand the concept. I envision my life as a train, set on railroad tracks, with an engine that makes it go. I see hope as the destination of the train. The tracks upon which the train moves are love, and the engine that makes it move is faith. The Apostle Paul referred to "Christ in you, the hope of glory" (Col. 1:27). When I see my own suffering as a way of sharing in Christ's suffering, I'm driven toward hope. I know that I have a "why," a reason for what I experience. Therefore, I have hope.

FINDING CHRIST'S PRESENCE IN SUFFERING

It is hard to put the presence of Christ into words. Sometimes it appears to be an incredible inner peace. At other times, it seems more like overwhelming joy. I've even heard people describe Christ's presence an unusual strength, both spiritual and physical. Sometimes the presence of Christ brings protection from harm. At other times, it brings unexpected words to a painful relationship, which result in healing. But could suffering be a manifestation of Christ's presence?

Christ is present in our suffering, and if we look for him, we will find him there. Often, our emotions and energy are so dulled by pain that we feel distant from God. At those times, we need others to remind us that God is near. Elie Weisel, a Holocaust survivor and historian, relates an incredible story of the presence of God in his book *Night*.

According to Weisel, two men and a boy were brought before all the prisoners in the Auschwitz concentration camp. Accused of sabotage, they were sentenced to death by hanging. The crowd stood silent and tense as a noose was placed around the neck of each man and the boy. Hundreds of prisoners watched in horror as an officer pulled the lever and the trapdoor of the gallows opened. Each man dropped instantly to his death. But not the boy. Because the apparatus was made for adults, the noose did not fit tightly around the neck of the child. As a result, he hung, writhing in agony, suspended between life and death. Weisel reports that from somewhere behind him, he kept hearing the whisper, "Where is God? Where is He?"

Then, Weisel says, "I heard a voice within me answer him; 'Where is He? Here He is—He is hanging here on this gallows.'"[11]

Scripture says about Jesus, "Although he was a son, he learned obedience from what he suffered and, once made perfect, he became the source of eternal salvation for all who obey him. . ." (Heb. 5:8–9). He became like us. He suffered with us. He is present in our suffering. This, then, is the ultimate hope: that God is with us, even in our pain. This is our blessing in the mundane suffering of a boring job, a difficult relationship, or a financial loss; and in the acute suffering of illness, persecution, and death: we have Christ in us, the hope of glory.

TO THINK ABOUT

1. What kinds of suffering have you experienced in your life?

2. How do you usually react to suffering?

3. Can you see any good that has come from your suffering?

4. Describe the ways in which you have felt Christ's presence while you were suffering.

THE BLESSING OF RECONCILIATION

*God's action is invisible to the world—
but the action of the community is visible.*
—Dietrich Bonhoeffer

Jan and George were newly married graduates of a Christian college when they attended a worship service at our church one Sunday morning. My husband, Wayne, is pastor to this multi-ethnic congregation in a suburb of Washington, D.C. He greeted the newcomers warmly, and they professed excitement about joining a church that displayed a vibrant mix of age, race, and culture. They spoke readily of their love for God and their desire to model their lives on the example of Jesus Christ. This eager pair returned to church for several weeks in a row and expressed an interest in serving in some ministry. Eventually, they made a commitment to serve as mentors for Fatu and Damba, teenagers whose families had recently emigrated from Africa. It was a challenging assignment because in addition to being from a foreign culture, the teens had a strong family Muslim influence.

But Jan and George accepted the role willingly, believing that God had called them to make an impact on the lives of these young women.

The mentoring sessions began around the end of September, and it seemed that the young couple was forming a good relationship with the teenage girls. Then, just before Halloween, George left a message on my husband's answering machine. "Pastor," George said, "we feel it's best for us to find another church."

Stunned by the news, my husband returned the call immediately. After a lengthy pause, George described the situation. He and Jan had found a church nearby that had lots of people like them—about the same age, from the same culture, and from a Christian tradition that was familiar to them. George and Jan liked being with these people, so they concluded that God had led them there.

"What about Fatu and Damba?" Wayne asked pointedly. "You believed that God had called you to mentor them."

"Well," George responded weakly, "we just feel like this is God's will."

As the call ended, it seemed obvious what had really happened. George and Jan began by pursuing the noble goal of helping two African teens find peace and comfort in a faith and a new land. They ended by pursuing their own peace and comfort.

When we broke the news to the families of Fatu and Damba, their parents seemed confused. They knew that their children were bright and eager to learn. They had been thrilled that a nice young couple would spend time with their children. It was difficult to explain to one of the fathers, a former government official who had been granted political asylum in the United States, why his daughter was suddenly dropped. Although the girls didn't say much, I feared that the damage from this incident would not be easily repaired. These young women had come from a war-torn country and had already a great deal of loss. If Christians broke their word to them, who could be trusted? Who would help them find their place in a strange land?

THE CHALLENGE OF RECONCILIATION

"It is God's will." Those words are used often—perhaps too often—by Christians when justifying a decision that smacks of self-interest. How refreshing it would be to hear a Christian say, for example when leaving a congregation, "I really don't like it here, and I'd like to try something different." It would be even better to see a serious attempt to resolve differences, to make peace, to reconcile. But running is always easier, and it seems that most Christians have a good pair of track shoes.

Yet Jesus said, "Blessed are the peacemakers, for they will be called children of God" (Matt. 5:9 NRSV). We are called to be peacemakers—reconcilers—in this world, and it is in doing so that we find God's blessing. Lisa Cahill picks up that challenge in her book *Love Your Enemies*. She writes: "If one is to go beyond merely self-gratifying relationships, then one must aim to be as perfect in the ways of mercy and forbearance. The morally right act is simply but radically the act that demonstrates the forgiving attentiveness to the needs of others disclosed by Jesus as the will of God."[1]

In our self-serving culture, it is difficult to see beyond the comfort of our small circle of relationships. So Jesus' teaching that we are blessed if we make peace suggests that we need a radical change. We need to be transformed by God's power if we are to move beyond our comfort zone and boldly practice reconciliation. God must change our hearts. Only that personal change, and the love that results, will sustain our attempts to make peace with others.

ACTION

There is a very real difference between peacekeeping and peacemaking. I first became aware of that distinction while observing the struggle for peace in Sierra Leone. This small country on the western coast of Africa had experienced brutal civil war for about ten years. Because of strong pressure from the international community, the United Nations finally sent a peacekeeping force to Sierra Leone in 1999. The arrival of these troops brought hope to the citizens, but peace did not follow. The peacekeepers were under strict orders not to engage in any kind of warfare. Their mission was simply to be there.

After a few weeks, the rebel faction took hundreds of the peacekeepers hostage. Soon random fighting broke out all over the country, particularly in the capital city of Freetown. The citizens were frantic. In the previous year, they had witnessed the nearly total destruction of their city and the massacre of thousands. They were determined that those events would not be repeated. In desperation, one government official in that country, which is more than 60 percent Muslim, requested that everyone should go to the streets at 6:00 P.M. and shout "Jesus!" That is exactly what happened. Thousands of people flooded the streets of Freetown with an amazing chorus of praise.

Before long, a British warship was seen in the harbor. A few days later, the British sent troops who were there as peace*makers*. They had authority to act. Soon, seventeen thousand U.N. soldiers were on the ground in Sierra Leone, the largest U.N. contingency in the world at that time. In a few months, rebels began to surrender their weapons, and the government turned them into hoes, picks, and shovels. I observed thousands of rebels exchanging their weapons for job skill training. I couldn't help but recall Isaiah's vision: "He will judge between the nations and will settle disputes for many peoples. They will beat their swords into plowshares and their spears into pruning hooks. Nation will not take up sword against nation, nor will they train for war anymore" (Isa. 2:4). This is a vision of God's kingdom.

By citing the example of Sierra Leone, I do not endorse

an aggressive or pro-war policy. I do believe, however, that peacemaking is an active thing. Even the nonviolent, passive resistance practiced by Gandhi and by Martin Luther King Jr. was very active. We do not make peace by doing nothing. We must take action in order to be reconciled.

CONFRONTATION

After a peace agreement was made in Sierra Leone, a Truth and Reconciliation Commission was established. The purpose was to reconcile former enemies by allowing both the victims and the perpetrators of violence to tell their stories. These stories were recorded in the hope that no such dastardly events would ever happen again in that country. One of the tactics of the Commission was to have victims and perpetrators come face to face to seek reconciliation. When making peace, it is necessary to confront the underlying issues that prevent reconciliation. To do so, peacemakers must risk upsetting relationships that are tolerable if not fully peaceful. That may happen on an individual as well as a national level.

I recall the evening, some twenty-five years ago, when the phone rang as our family was sitting down for dinner. Wayne took the call, and I saw a cloud of concern come over his face. He listened for a moment or two, then responded gravely: "I will be right over." As he walked out the door, my husband called over his shoulder: "The police are on their way to Lanny and Kaye's house. He's holding her at gunpoint. Their oldest daughter just phoned from the neighbor's." He paused a moment. "Pray for me."

Lanny was a hot-tempered man who became violent when he drank. He had married Kaye, his third wife, with the hope that this time things would "work out." The couple had been attending church, which Lanny saw as a kind of magic cure. But a lifelong pattern of controlling situations and people with anger cannot be easily changed. As Wayne arrived on the scene, the police were leading Lanny away in

141

handcuffs. He screamed obscenities at Kaye as she stood on the porch with her three children. The police advised her to find another place to stay that night, someplace unknown to Lanny. It was likely that he would post bail within a few hours and be released. He would certainly come looking for her.

Blindly gathering clothes and belongings, Kaye and the children left their comfortable house for a small motel room. Sure enough, Lanny did post bail and was back at their home in about six hours. He angrily phoned our home, demanding to know Kaye's whereabouts. I took the call and honestly told him that I had no idea where she was.

In the days that followed, Kaye did some radical peace-making. She realized that in order to be reconciled to Lanny, she would have to confront the underlying problems in their lives. She refused to yield to Lanny's angry demands and arranged to live with her children in an undisclosed place until a restraining order could be obtained against him. For his part, Lanny had to scramble to find a place to live so that he could continue working. The only place he could find was the basement of a friend's house. Life wasn't terribly pleasant for Lanny, and the reality of his situation began to dawn on him.

In time, we began to see changes in Lanny. He started to pray more frequently and more openly, he began to study Scripture with some men from the church, and he attended anger management classes. Meanwhile, Kaye and the children returned home, where she held her ground. She began attending a support group for spouses of alcoholics and began to study Scripture more attentively. Kaye began to value herself as a person created in the image of God. Lanny and Kaye would see each other at church on Sunday morning. They would talk while others were around, then go their separate ways. Both of them accepted the fact that there would be no quick fix to their relationship.

After about six months, Lanny and Kaye reunited. They continued to grow in their faith, and after several years

Lanny chose to study for the ministry. When he completed his studies, he joined the staff of a church, where he and Kaye have ministered effectively to many families. In fact their children are now serving in the ministry as well. As I recall that pivotal night so many years ago, I wonder what might have happened if Kaye had not been willing to confront the issues that prevented peace. Who knows what might have become of them all? But because Kaye was willing to take action, this family truly knows the blessing of reconciliation.

Lanny and Kaye's may be an extreme case, but nearly every family has relationships that need to be mended. There, in the family, is the greatest need for reconciliation. It is in the family that people can learn to be reconciled, and when they do, the ripple effect of peacemaking will spread to schools, workplaces, communities, and even governments. But before that can happen, someone must be willing to face the issues and take action.

ELEMENTS OF RECONCILIATION

The Hebrew word for peace, *shalom,* has a meaning broader than our English term. Shalom means wholeness, unity, and balance. The Bible begins with an example of shalom, the creation of order from chaos, and shalom is the last image in the book of Revelation, John's vision of all nations worshiping the Lord God in unity and harmony. Most Christians see that peaceful state as something that God will create sometime in the future. In fact, that vision is an imperative for all of Christ's followers NOW! Shalom is the theme of the Scriptures from beginning to end, and we are to take part in making that vision a present reality. We are to be agents of reconciliation, agents of peace.

Shalom, biblical reconciliation, is a complex thing. It has economic, social, and spiritual dimensions. To achieve true peace—wholeness, unity, and balance—requires setting things right not only with God but also with others. When that happens, justice and mercy will characterize our relationships, and our needs will give way to the needs of others. On a trip to Haiti, I was presented with a wooden bell that bore this inscription: "The cry of the poor is like this wooden bell; it rings but no one listens." The road to reconciliation begins when we listen to the wooden bell, taking the needs of others as seriously as we take our own.

HONESTY

In his book *Streams of Living Water,* Richard Foster eloquently describes the political and spiritual situation in the time of the prophet Jeremiah. Foster writes:

> Jeremiah lamented the fraud and greed of his day, saying, "They have treated the wound of my people carelessly, saying 'Peace, peace,' when there is no peace" (6:14). In essence, Jeremiah had filed a malpractice suit against self-styled religious quacks. They had put a Band-Aid over a gaping social wound and said, "*Shalom, shalom*—all is well." But Jeremiah thundered back, "*En-shalom*— all is not well. Justice is spurned, the poor are oppressed, the orphan is ignored. There is no wholeness, no healing here!"[2]

Jeremiah was the lone prophet who had the courage to speak the truth about his generation. He was willing to name the elephant in the room, speaking plainly about the lack of wholeness, unity, and balance in his society. Jeremiah told the truth about injustice, and that is never an easy task.

Yet even as Jeremiah decried the injustice of his day, he believed that healing would come. He looked forward to a new day when God would make a new covenant with his people. God had told Jeremiah, "I will put my law within

144

them, and I will write it on their hearts; and I will be their God, and they shall be my people. No longer shall they teach one another, or say to each other, 'Know the Lord,' for they shall all know me, from the least of them to the greatest, says the Lord; for I will forgive their iniquity, and remember their sin no more" (Jer. 31:33–34).

COURAGE

Reconciliation begins with interpersonal relationships but must encompass community relationships as well. An early threat to the unity and harmony of the early church arose when the widows of Greek-speaking Jews were left out of the church's daily food distribution (see Acts 6:1–7). These widows had no income and were entirely dependent on the charity of the community. Because the Greek-speakers were an ethnic minority, the situation had the potential to become an explosive controversy. Church leaders might have dallied in analyzing the reason for the discrimination, rationalized some facile explanation, or ignored the problem entirely. Instead, they listened to the cry of the poor and addressed the situation immediately, appointing seven deacons to supervise the distribution of food. It is important to note that all seven of the deacons had Greek names (Acts 6:5). The leaders of the early church had both the wisdom and the courage to share their power, placing members of the minority group in these positions of responsibility. They pursued peace through compassion.

The words *compassion* and *reconciliation* may sound soft and sentimental, but the reality of compassion ministry is not soft at all. It involves the confrontation of evil structures, which demands courage and perseverance. People who engage in this form of ministry must be full of "God's grace and power," as was Stephen, a leader in the early church's compassion ministry (Acts 6:8). Stephen addressed the issue of injustice with both words and actions, performing many miraculous signs and wonders. I wonder, do we expect God to work in a mighty way as we approach the problems of poverty, homelessness, and hunger in our communities? Do we expect God to perform miracles in a homeless shelter or to give signs of his power at a local food pantry? Do we even bother to pray about such things. It's possible that the only prayers said by those engaging in ministries of compassion are prayers for their own safety as they visit undesirable parts the city.

I do remember one prayer, however, given by a saintly woman named Mrs. Smith in the inner city in Washington, D.C., during the 1970s. She led the work at the soup kitchen in the Sojourners community. She prayed: "Lord, I know you will be coming through this line today. Help us to treat you good." If we prayed in that spirit, I believe we would see signs and wonders in our soup kitchens, homeless shelters, and food pantries. Perhaps this is the very prayer that Stephen prayed.

I don't think it's a coincidence that the first Christian martyr was a leader in the church's compassion ministry. Both the work that Stephen did and the manner in which he did it were a threat to the Jews—the majority group of that time. He was placed on trial under false charges and then put to death by stoning (Acts 7). Stephen was an eloquent speaker, and as the stones were hurled that would crush the life from his body, he offered these last words, the ultimate expression of shalom: "Lord, do not hold this sin against them."

No, there is nothing soft or sentimental about the ministry of reconciliation.

RISK

Attacking social evil is always risky. That was certainly true when godly people opposed the institution of human slavery both in North America and in Great Britain. At first, some people sought to avoid the issue by appealing to Scripture. After all, the Bible seems to legitimize slavery by offering rules for the conduct of slaves (Eph. 6:5–9). Others thought they could solve the problem by seeing that slaves were properly fed and clothed. In the end, it became evident that the entire practice of slavery was evil and needed to be confronted.

Much of the credit for exposing this evil goes to Christians, such as those of the Clapham parish, and Anglican congregation of mostly wealthy and titled people in eighteenth century England. William Wilberforce, the leading opponent of slavery in the British parliament, was a member of the Clapham Parish. The leaders of this group spent three hours in prayer each day and united Christians all over England in prayer on the eve of important debates in parliament.[3] British Christians confronted the evil of slavery in many ways, including civil disobedience of the Fugitive Slave Law of 1793. This law was intended to prohibit people from helping runaway slaves. Many believers, notably the Quakers, ignored the law at great personal risk.

The war against slavery was a long and costly struggle. It was seen as an attack on the financial base of the British Empire, and abolitionists were depicted as advocates of financial ruin. Some leaders lost their health and their fortunes in the fight. Yet in 1807, the bill that effectively ended slavery in Great Britain was passed by a vote of 283 to 16. In 1833 slave owners were given one year to release their slaves and were compensated a total of twenty million pounds by the English treasury, a rare and righteous act by a government.[4]

Later, abolitionists in the United States followed a similar path by boldly confronting that evil in their society. I have visited the homes of Wesleyan Methodists in Michigan who were leaders in the abolitionist movement. Their houses, now museums, had secret rooms and passageways for hiding fugitive slaves. The abolitionists realized the high risk they were taking. If caught, they could be heavily fined or even imprisonment. Yet their faith called them to a higher level of peacemaking—a higher blessing. They were willing to confront the injustice of their day, and powerful changes resulted. As Donald Bloesch has observed, "The Gospel is a stick of dynamite in the social structure."[5]

Today, we continue to struggle with the implications of the gospel for racial reconciliation. I have been present for many discussions of this issue by groups of mixed race, and I know that the prejudices that we have learned over the years run deep. Yet I have learned that forming genuine friendships helps to diminish the distance between people of different races. On the macro level, however, racial reconciliation involves the issue of power. I have participated in church services that included important but largely symbolic ceremonies of repentance, foot washing, and forgiveness seeking. Unfortunately, when the time came to take the next step, reorganizing unjust structures and sharing power, the reconciliation process stopped. Reconciliation always involves risk, and many Christians have a low risk tolerance.

BARRIERS TO RECONCILIATION

If the abolitionists of the eighteenth and nineteenth centuries needed a great deal of courage, at least they had an obvious target for their peacemaking efforts. The situation today is somewhat different. How do we make peace in a Christian community that is divided by personality, power, and opinion rather than by obvious violations of scriptural principles? This is certainly the challenge today, and Paul addresses it in his letter to the Christians in Rome: "Live in harmony with one another" he writes, then lists principles for doing just that. "Do not be proud, but be willing to associate with people of low position. Do not be conceited" (Rom. 12:16). The ego continues to be a vexing obstacle for peacemakers.

EGO
When our children were old enough to be left alone for an hour or two, Wayne and I would place one of them

in charge of the others. We made sure to rotate the assignment so that the eldest child was not "the boss" every time. It was always interesting to note the behavior of the most recent boss. For several days afterward, the child would carry the aura of that short-lived power. Eventually, another sibling would bring him or her down in some way.

The temptation to lord authority over others or to get even is a problem both in the Christian community and in the world. Paul gives pointed instructions on the matter of living in harmony with others in Rom. 12:18–21: "Do not repay any evil for evil. Be careful to do what is right in the eyes of everybody. If it is possible as far as it depends on you live at peace with everyone. Do not take revenge, my friend, but leave room for God's wrath." He concludes with this radical advice: "If your enemy is hungry, feed him; If he is thirsty, give him something to drink. . . . Do not be overcome by evil, but overcome evil with good".

On the surface, this kind of peacemaking sounds passive; but it is the essence of reconciliation, and there is nothing weak about it. It can only be done through the strength and courage that comes from knowing Christ. I often wonder how the church would be perceived by the world if Christians consistently followed this radical advice. What would happen if planeloads of food were delivered to enemy states? What hinders the church from doing so? What hinders you and me?

FEAR

Perhaps the greatest barrier is fear. What would happen if I were to suddenly begin caring for those who have slandered me? Wouldn't that give them the very power that they've been seeking? What happens if they win? Would God protect me? Can I really trust him to do the right thing? Is his Word reliable?

I would like to say that I have no trouble in this area and am constantly at peace in my relationships. But that is not the case. I do not enjoy destructive criticism, particularly from Christian brothers and sisters. When criticized, my first response, based on fear, is to become defensive and avoid the issue. Generally, when a confrontation does comes, I look for the weakness in the other person, my "enemy." That is the beginning of a downward spiral that leads to anger, depression, broken relationships, and self-doubt. Thankfully, I have learned to deny that initial impulse and practice the principle of overcoming evil with good. In the process, I experience peacemaking in new ways through the power of Jesus Christ.

UNFORGIVENESS

Reconciliation and forgiveness are always integrated. You cannot have one without the other. That means the road to reconciliation is a long one. Library shelves are crowded with books on forgiveness. The sheer volume of material is one indication of how difficult it is to forgive. Yet the Scripture gives us both a strong call to forgive one another and the assurance that it can be done. Jesus modeled that forgiveness throughout his life and especially at the moment of his death, and the Holy Spirit gives us the wisdom and power to be reconciled to those who have hurt us. Forgiveness is the key that unlocks one of God's richest blessings.

LEADERSHIP

Even if I have the teaching of Scripture and clear examples in history, how do I begin to bring about reconciliation in my church or community? Perhaps the church board and the pastor are at odds over a new building. Imagine that I am not on the board but am an active member of the church. As a stay-at-home mom, I receive a lot of calls concerning the conflict. The conflict is spilling into the broader community and damaging the church's reputation. I'm deeply concerned, but I don't want to get involved in something that is none of my business.

That is not an uncommon scenario. The fear of taking sides is one of the greatest obstacles to becoming a peacemaker. But

I've found that God often uses the most unlikely people to bring the blessing of reconciliation to a community. It is often the "outsiders" who are able to bring a fresh look at Scripture and remind the "players" that the work of God is spiritual, not political.

That applies beyond the church as well. The world is crying for leaders who will bring reconciliation to ethnic groups and social classes. Gender differences, regional prejudice, and political ideology are barriers to reconciliation. There is a great need for men and women to step forward in the name of Jesus Christ and become ministers of reconciliation. The blessing of reconciliation is not a task only for specially trained leaders. Each of us may be a minister of reconciliation.

Recently I heard of a situation in which the relationship between some Christians was broken over the issue of educating children. Some were convinced that home schooling was best, others believed in sending their children to private schools, and still others favored public school education. As I heard the comments that had been made by each group, I realized that education had become a secondary issue; they had begun to question one another's faith, integrity, and worth. They needed a leader to step forward in a spirit of humility and become an agent of reconciliation. How many similar conflicts occur each day in families, churches, workplaces, and even nations? How many could be avoided or resolved if someone would take the initiative to become an agent of reconciliation?

THE BLESSING OF RECONCILIATION

Following my visit to the Toul Sleng prison in Cambodia, the former torture chamber of the Khmer Rouge, I sat in the very small living room of a tiny apartment in Phnom Penh along with ten new converts to Christianity. As our meeting began, each person shared his or her story.

151

Mr. Chinn was an art professor at the university who had survived the Khmer Rouge reign of terror. He said that during the 1970s, the Khmer Rouge had planned to kill all the university professors. Chinn was frightened for his life but had no place to run. "I just hoped they would not find me," he said sheepishly, "but they did." He continued:

> One night the door opened, and I knew my time had come. A soldier came over to me, put a gun to my head, and began shouting at me. I had the fleeting thought, *I have heard of this Jesus, I wonder if he could help me.* So I just prayed under my breath, 'Jesus, help me!'
>
> At that moment the soldier pulled the trigger with the gun held against my temple, but the gun did not fire. Again he pulled the trigger, and again it did not fire. Finally, after the third time, the soldier cursed, threw the gun on the ground, and ran. Then I knew that Jesus is the Living God.

Sitting next to Mr. Chinn was a man named Mr. Chun. "My story is very different," Mr. Chun began, his eyes cast toward the floor. "I was a member of the Khmer Rouge. I was convinced that we could gain power and rule the country the way we wanted. We were poor, and they promised us wealth and power if we could get rid of the ruling class. I did many evil things." Chun paused, tears forming in his eyes. "After awhile I realized that this fighting was going nowhere; I knew there had to be a better way. But I did not think I could ever be forgiven for what I had done. But thanks to the people in this room who told me about Jesus, I have been forgiven, and I am clean."

When Mr. Chun had finished speaking, the two men looked at each other, then embraced, tears rolling down their cheeks. Jesus was the bridge to reconciliation between these former enemies. The blessing of peace was evident in the room that night.

We went on to discuss the hopes of the Cambodian people. Clean water was near the top of the list. Sixty-four percent of the people in Cambodia do not have access to clean water. Mr Chun suggested that, because the Cambodian people need both water and the gospel, we should dig a well in every place that we plant a church. The group readily agreed. As a result, living water and spiritual water are both flowing throughout Cambodia. The reconciliation between those former enemies is generating life and hope for thousands.

Being reconciled is never easy, for it is not friends but enemies who must engage in the process. The task is daunting. As followers of Jesus Christ, we depend on him to bring success. He is the giver of this blessing, and he will enable us to do whatever is required to receive it. The Apostle Paul puts it this way:

> We don't evaluate people by what they have or how they look. . . . we look inside, and what we see is that anyone united with the Messiah gets a fresh start. . . . All this comes from the God who settled the relationship between us and him, and then called us to settle our relationships with each other. God put the world square with himself through the Messiah, giving the world a fresh start by offering forgiveness of sins. God has given us the task of telling everyone what he is doing. We're Christ's representatives. God uses us to persuade men and women to drop their differences and enter into God's work of making things right between them. We're speaking for Christ himself now: Become friends with God: he's already a friend with you (2 Cor. 5:16–21 The Message).

Can a former political prisoner and a former torturer become partners in bringing new life to a divided nation?

Why not? If God can forgive you and me, anything is possible. When we put that thought into action by offering to others the same forgiveness we have received, we give the whole world a fresh start. Who knows where that might lead?

TO THINK ABOUT

1. In what relationships do you now need reconciliation? As you look around your community, your church, and your nation, do you see areas where reconciliation is needed? Between whom?

2. What hinders you from becoming a leader in the ministry of reconciliation?

3. Imagine the changes that might happen in your life, in your community, and throughout the world if genuine reconciliation were to take place. What might it be like?

4. Name something you can do to pursue reconciliation.

CHAPTER EIGHT

The Blessing of Possibility

*At the end of the twentieth century,
we are engaged in a process through which God
is ending our "known world" and inviting
us to a new world of obedience and praise.*
—Walter Brueggemann

With blonde curls encircling her fair-skinned face and blue eyes sparkling with excitement, five-year-old Halley was a picture of hope as she sang enthusiastically, "I am a promise, I am a possibility, I am a promise with a capital *P,* I can be anything, anything He wants me to be."

In the mid-1980s, many children were singing that song, but when Halley sang it, tears welled up in my eyes; I knew that this precious child had lived a hard life. She and her two older siblings had been made wards of the court after witnessing the murder of their mother by their father. They were placed in foster care with Shirley and David, a loving couple who worked for a children's home. Halley enjoyed accompanying Shirley and David as they traveled, representing the home to churches all over the country. The irrepressible pre-schooler loved to sing, and the song seemed to have been written especially for her.

As I listened to the lyrics, I thought about what the words might mean for Halley's future. It struck me that this precious child had already received one of the greatest of God's blessings: she had hope.

THE NATURE OF HOPE

Hope is a rare commodity in this world. That was perhaps more true in the mid-1960s, when the works of Jürgen Moltmann were translated into English. To a culture steeped in nihilism and the death of God theology, this German theologian's work came as a breath of fresh air. His book *Theology of Hope* created an immediate sensation. In it, Moltmann describes God as a God of hope, a God with a future. What's more, Moltmann says, faith and hope, are inextricably connected. There is no hope without faith and vice versa.

> Faith believes God to be true, hope awaits the time when this truth shall be manifested; faith believes that he is our Father, hope anticipates that he will ever show himself to be a father toward us; faith believes that eternal life has been given to us, hope anticipates that it will some time be revealed; faith is the foundation upon which hope rests, hope nourishes and sustains faith.[1]

Without hope, Moltmann concludes, "faith falls to pieces." It becomes fainthearted and, ultimately, dead. This may be the reason that hope is often modified by an adjective in Scripture. The Bible refers to hope or those who have it as joyful (Rom. 12:12), righteous (Gal. 5:5), glorious (Col. 1:27), patient (1 Thess 1:3) blessed (Titus 2:13), and lively (1 Pet. 1:2). Hope is a vibrant, living thing.

SMALL BEGINNINGS

If hope is in fact a part of God's nature, then as we take on his likeness, we must become hopeful. Paul speaks of us gaining Christ's righteousness (Rom. 4); hope must be a part of that character transformation. Jesus exemplified hope in his life and taught it repeatedly in his parables. To know Christ is to have hope.

In Mark, chapter 4, three of Jesus' parables are recorded, each having to do with agriculture. That subject was familiar to Jesus' hearers; he was speaking directly to their experience. His point, however, took them beyond the physical task of growing food into the discovery of a spiritual truth. In these parables, Jesus particularly emphasized how small seeds are and how long they take to grow. Every person who heard Jesus understood the truth of that. Yet when he applied those observations to the kingdom of God, the crowd must have been puzzled. In those days, the word *kingdom* necessarily referred to something grand and powerful. Even today, it is sometimes hard to think of the kingdom of God as something growing slowly and secretly. Yet that was Jesus' message. The Kingdom is based on hope.

The person who sows a seed hopes it will grow—knows it will—but must be patient as the tiny germ slowly sprouts and takes root. In the same way, good things often start small in our lives. But we have faith; therefore we have hope that greater things will follow. Jesus taught us that God has possibilities beyond our imagination. The kingdom of God—the seed—is the inner power of possibility. It is interesting that these parables all have to do with summer- and springtime activities; fall and winter happenings are not mentioned. God is the God of creation, the God of new life. With him, there is always a spring.

GREAT POSSIBILITIES

Can something that begins so small truly turn into something grand and beautiful? Is there hope, for example, that anything we do might lead to a solution for the pandemic of AIDS in Africa? I believe it will. God wants to use ordinary people who have passion and hope to heal that suffering continent.

As I traveled the rough roads of Zambia in the summer of 2002, for the first time I touched the people behind the statistics I'd read. It was a powerful experience. The words of a mother from Pemba still ring in my ears. She told of her husband's death, the debt her family had incurred, and the heart-rending decision she had made in order to feed her children. Beating herself with a clenched fist, she cried, "Against my own will, against my faith, I became a prostitute." With tears streaming down her thin face, she said, "AIDS kills in years. But hunger kills within days." At those words, my mind raced to my own four children, and I wondered, *What would I have done in her place?*

Zambia has been called the cradle of Africa's AIDS crisis.[2] Of Zambia's 11.5 million people, 5 percent, roughly 575,000, are AIDS orphans, children who have lost one or both parents to this disease.[3] A full 46 percent of all households in Zambia care for orphans; some experts claim that number is as high as 75 percent.[4]

Facts like those rolled easily off my tongue until I visited a rural community church near the town of Zimba. The pastor there had arranged for us to meet community people and hear their stories. He led us along a path lined with elephant grass as high as our heads until we came to a clearing. There stood a neat mud-brick church and beside it, a group of children, teens, and older people, eagerly awaiting our arrival. After polite curtseys from the children and handshakes from the adults, we made our way into the cool building. We took our seats on log benches, and sitting on the first three rows was a group of children, all dressed in their finest, with clothes clean and hair groomed. The pastor pointed to them and explained that all twenty-five of them were AIDS orphans.

On the opposite side of the room, an elderly gentleman rose to his feet. Speaking in English, he stated that he was eighty-four years old and that all of his children had died from the "crisis." He himself was taking care of nine orphans. Then a teenager stood and pointed to all the brothers and sisters who were left in her care when both of their parents had died. A very thin woman stood and pointed to the number of children she cared for in addition to her own. Suddenly, the numbers became faces. I was overwhelmed by the magnitude of this crisis.

Yet at the same moment, hope welled within me. Within a few moments, we began planning an income-generating project for that community, which would assist them in caring for the orphans. We also made plans for a program to train caregivers and for improvements in education, initiatives that would benefit the entire community. Hope began to rise within the children as they realized they would not have to be moved from their community and placed in a strange environment. The fulfillment of this hope will involve people from many walks of life, each investing time, resources, skill, and prayer, but the seed has been planted. Who knows what may result? World Hope International now plans to provide care for twenty-five thousand AIDS orphans over the next three years through this community-based approach.

ENDLESS POSSIBILITIES

In Luke, chapter 15, we find another group of parables, these having to do with the experience of losing and finding. Jesus spoke of a lost sheep, a lost coin, and a lost son. Everyone can identify with the experience of losing and finding a valuable item. When searching for something that has been lost, a person may become totally absorbed in the task. One is liable to retrace steps and strain to recall every moment of time since the item was last seen. The intense anxiety felt over losing something of value is matched only by the great joy of finding it.

These are universal and timeless feelings, and Jesus relates them to the kingdom of God. When we finally discover the Kingdom, it brings great joy. Life becomes filled with new possibilities. Moltman describes the kingdom of God as the "open, vast space in which we can develop because there are no more limitations in it. If we experience the kingdom of God in this way, then we once again perceive the fullness of our life possibilities."[5]

In telling these parables, Jesus invited his listeners to imagine a world that was limited neither by secular Roman rule nor the religious law of the Jews but was alive with possibilities. The stories are open ended. Jesus never dictated twelve principles for finding new life or six steps to successful living. Instead, he motivated listeners to let go of the present reality and look to a better one. The result, Jesus promises, will be joy.

Martin Luther King Jr. eloquently articulated this vision of hope in his famous sermon "I Have a Dream." King didn't give a list of ten points for creating a just society. Instead, he aroused the imagination of an oppressed community. He lifted up a dream. That dream raised hope within his listeners. That hope convinced them that things would not stay as they were; there would be a new social reality. As a result, many people were willing to let go of the comfort of the present and work toward a better future.

I often remember five-year-old Halley singing her hope-filled song so many years ago. Sometimes I imagine her now, thinking of the pain of her past life, recalling the unspeakable tragedy that she witnessed. That pain is still there, I am sure. Yet it must be remembered in a new context—in the light of hope. For Halley, possibility became reality. That happens every day for those who have hope. Out of the ashes of injustice, oppression, and suffering grows the tiny seed of new life. The Kingdom has come.

THE CHALLENGE OF HOPE

The statistics always alarm me. There are roughly six billion people in the world, and four billion are what is known as the Two-Thirds World, the world's poor.[6] Every year six million children die before their fifth birthday because of chronic hunger and related diseases.[7] Some 800 million people are undernourished.[8] At the same time, Christianity is the largest religion in the world. In spite of that, poverty grinds on. When I speak of poverty, I mean not only the want of food, clothing, or shelter but also the lack of education and opportunity. Our culture enjoys the myth that people are poor because they want to be. Another deception is that poor people are fools. We, particularly Christians, tend to look down on the poor believing that they are lazy or stupid.

That attitude is contrary to both the teaching of Scripture and the life of Jesus. It appears that Christianity in the West has become so intertwined with the American Dream that we are simply blind to the claims of Scripture. Yet if we are to take the theology of hope seriously, we must accept the challenge of hope. We must take stock of our world and do what we must to bring God's blessing to others.

GREAT POTENTIAL

Whenever I pray as our Lord taught us, "your kingdom come on earth as it is in heaven," I wonder what the world would be like if we dared to hope that this prayer would be answered. What would happen if we dared to create a new reality, the New Kingdom that Jesus called for? What if we dared to act on that possibility? We catch some glimpses of what might result in history. John and Charles Wesley, for example, succeeded in launching a great revival in which the cause of justice was advanced in England in the eighteenth century.

Moltmann says that "Christianity is completely and entirely and utterly hope, a looking forward, and a forward direction; hope is not just an appendix. . . . Therefore, it is a

163

setting forth and a transformation of the present. It makes the Church the source of continual new impulses towards the realization of righteousness, freedom and humanity here in the light of the promised future that is to come."[9] Hope is more than just a wistful fantasy. It is an imperative. We not only can but must bring the Kingdom to earth.

Each year since 1997, *The New York Times* has asked a handful of academics to offer their suggestions for the most overrated and underrated ideas ever produced. The 2002 lists were intriguing. The first list was titled "Out with the Overrated," and included such bizarre notions as the facial transplant. The second list, "In with the Underrated," was headed by a fascinating entry: Christianity. The text explained:

> The most underrated force in global affairs is Christianity. It is by far the world's largest religion, and it will continue to hold this position into the foreseeable future; but few of us notice how the character of that faith is being transformed. Over the past century, Christian numbers have been booming in the global south, in Africa, Asia and Latin America. For example, since 1900, the number of African Christians has grown spectacularly from around 10 million to over 360 million. Just within my baby-boomer lifetime, "Western Christianity" has become ever less significant as the faith's center of gravity has shifted.

> And as Christianity has been, so to speak, going south, the religion has been adapting very rapidly to the cultures in which it operates. We see an upsurge of charismatic and supernatural-oriented forms of belief and practice. The emergence of southern Christianity constitutes a religious and cultural revolution quite comparable to the Reformation of the sixteenth century, though on a far vaster scale.[10]

GREAT RESOURCES

As I read about phenomenal growth of Christianity in Africa, I'm startled by the irony of the situation. Africa is a continent with great poverty, illness, injustice, and political unrest. At the same time, it is a continent of great hospitality, having tremendous natural resources. Why hasn't the rise of Christianity brought justice, peace, and hope to this troubled land? Doesn't evangelism mean good news for the poor?

I believe it will be if discipleship becomes a priority in the church. Typically, Christians are more interested in making converts to the religion than disciples of Jesus Christ. Discipleship—becoming like Christ—involves far more than memorizing Scripture verses or attending church. True discipleship includes alleviating the problems of ignorance, poverty, hunger, racism, and other forms of oppression (see Amos 5:21; Luke 3:10–14, 4:18–21).

Is it possible to imagine a world filled with disciples? Bryant Myers, in his book *Walking with the Poor*, gives a comprehensive picture of how this type of discipleship would look. Myers describes the kingdom of God as a pyramid with each corner representing one aspect of the gospel:

- Being Being formed into the likeness of Christ.

- Word Teaching, preaching, and doing theology.

- Deed Working for the physical, social, psychological, and economic well-being of God's world.

- Sign Seeing miracles, the things that only God can do as well as the things the church does as a living sign of the kingdom.[11]

Myers goes on to discuss the role of nonpoor Christians in these contexts:

> The nonpoor Christian witness must include an invitation to lay down their God-complexes and turn over to God those roles that are rightfully God's. Christian witness means a call to exercise leadership as stewards who think more highly of others than themselves. Leaders with a biblical worldview know that all power belongs to God and that they exercise power only as stewards, not as owners or masters. Of those who have more, more is expected.[12]

Christianity is already the largest religion in the world. Perhaps when more Christians become serious about living as Jesus lived, we will see the Kingdom come in greater measure. That's my hope.

GREAT RESPONSIBILITIES

"To whom much is given, much is required." Those words, which echo the teaching of Jesus from Luke 12:48, rung in my ears. Jesus made a nearly identical statement about the use of money, so it was interesting to hear those words from the leader of the wealthiest nation on earth.

Shortly after our family moved to the Washington, D.C., area, I received an invitation from then President Bill Clinton to attend a breakfast in the State Dining Room of the White House. I am not sure how my name made it onto that the list for that memorable event. The invitation was addressed to "religious leaders," which included representatives from most religions in the United States. The topic was the state of the world's poor. The morning of the breakfast arrived, and I got up extra early. I certainly didn't want to be stuck in traffic and miss the occasion. What a story that would have made for my grandchildren. "Grandma was invited to visit the President . . . but she never made it off the beltway!"

I didn't need to worry; I was out well ahead of the morning rush hour traffic and arrived at the White House in plenty of time. After our group was seated, Mr. Clinton entered the room with all of the pomp and circumstance that generally accompanies the President of the United States. He greeted us, then began his speech about the state of the world. In his speech, the President described his dream that every child in the world would be able to have a meal every day and to go to school. He stated that the dream was not impossible because the resources exist in the world, particularly in the United States, to accomplish it. The President stated that he and Secretary of Agriculture Dan Glickman were working to make that dream a reality.

Several times during his speech, Mr. Clinton included these words: "To whom much is given, much is required." The last time he quoted that Scripture, the President emphasized its personal meaning. He said, "I just can't get away from [those words]" In spite of Mr. Clinton's well-publicized personal failures, it seemed that morning as if God's call continued to be upon his conscience. A similar call has long been upon my own heart.

John Wesley had a vision of "overturning the kingdom of evil and setting up the kingdom of Christ." The President had a dream to feed and educate every child in the world. We have been given great resources, and we have been given an even greater blessing—the hope that this dream may become reality. We are responsible for what we have.

GREAT OPPORTUNITIES

This grand vision seems out of reach for a local community, yet the Kingdom begins with a single seed. Great things come from small beginnings.

I was startled by a fact cited by an official at the Department of Health and Human Services. She stated that the majority of teenage mothers become pregnant between the hours of 3:00 and 5:00 P.M. That's because teens are often left alone during those hours—after school and before parents arrive home from work. Teenage pregnancy might be greatly reduced if churches and community groups would host mentoring programs, homework clubs, or other after-school activities. An added benefit would be the relationships developed between adults and teens, which would provide healthy role models for the young people. What might happen if just one person in your community became concerned enough about this problem to take action?

Hunger continues to be pervasive in our country and around the world. I have seen the effects of hunger up close—the swollen bellies of children who have had nothing to eat and the anguished expressions of parents who have watched their children die of starvation. This is the kingdom of evil, and it can be overturned. Bread for the World, a nationwide Christian citizens' movement, offers this hope-filled assessment:

> World hunger can be ended. We have already made significant progress. Thirty years ago there were 959,000,000 undernourished people in the developing world. Today there are 791,400,000 people in spite of a 2 billion rise in population. . . . It is feasible to reduce the number of undernourished people worldwide 50 percent by 2015. The cost would be an additional 4 billion per year, of which 1 billion would come from the United States.[13]

It is estimated that once the 2015 goal is met, the movement may generate enough momentum to end world hunger by 2030. The primary strategies employed in this effort are to improve livelihoods, to invest in health care, and to educate and empower people to participate in decisions that affect their lives. To do those things is to value people as bearers of God's image, for Jesus reminds us that when we feed and clothe others, we do it to him (see Matt. 25:31–46). Can you imagine what might result if every Christian took that thought seriously?

Sex trafficking is an evil that seems very far removed from our comfortable North American lives. Yet every year, more than four million women and children are sold into modern forms of slavery, primarly the sex trade,[14] and it is estimated that this vile trade is becoming more profitable than drug dealing. I recall seeing a film in which an investigator with a hidden camera entered a brothel and recorded the owner using all her wiles to sell a five-year-old child for sex. My stomach turned at the sight. Several months later, I saw another picture of that same child, this time smiling in her new setting, an aftercare home for children rescued from the sex trade. The child had been saved and the brothel owner brought to justice. Sex trafficking is a problem that must be addressed at many levels—public policy making, lobbying, enforcing laws, and caring for rescued children. Somewhere in that list may be something that you could do to bring hope to one of "the least of these."

In the summer of 2003, I had the honor of meeting some of these redeemed children and young women in Phnom Penh, Cambodia. One of the most profound experiences of my life was to have them lay hands on and pray for me. This was done at their request. You see, they have come to understand the depth of God's miraculous grace in a way that I still do not.

I could list many more opportunities to work for the Kingdom, but these few may be enough to ignite the imagination and prompt you to follow the Holy Spirit's lead in establishing the kingdom of Christ. Paul told the Christians in Rome to be joyful in hope (Rom. 12:12). Jesus told a parable about the Kingdom in which a man discovers a buried treasure and is filled with great joy (Matt. 13:44). How can one look at the grinding, debilitating problems of the world and be joyful? It is because we have hope, and that hope fires the imagination with endless possibilities for good.

HOPE BECOMES REALITY

I belong to one of several denominations that traces its heritage to the leadership of John Wesley, the eighteenth-century revivalist. Wesley was a tireless leader who believed that the power of God could transform both individuals and society. I've always been compelled by that vision. At the same time, I am chagrinned by how far churches in the Wesleyan family have departed from it. Even so, Wesley's example continues to inspire people. Tony Campolo, a university professor known for his dynamic speaking style and radical call to social justice and evangelism, cites his discovery of Wesley as one of the pivotal moments in his life. Campolo says, "Reading Wesley's description of his Aldersgate experience was a transforming experience for me. Out of this conversion grows the great Wesleyan revival with all of its social consciousness, attacking slavery, championing the rights of women, ending child labor laws. The Wesleyan vision was warmhearted evangelism with an incredible social vision. Trying to see the world as he saw it changed me greatly."[15]

Trying to see the world as Wesley saw it has greatly changed me also. But when I embraced the Wesleyan ideal of social transformation, I had no idea that this dream would take me to six continents of the globe and result in the founding of a worldwide relief and development organization.

VISION

For as long as I can remember, I have longed to see the Wesleyan dream realized. Seeing the conditions in our inner cities and witnessing the poverty and oppression in places like Ethiopia, Nicaragua, and El Salvador only fanned my passion to make a difference in the world. In 1974 I attended a conference that added a vision to that passion.

In 1973 Ron Sider brought together a cadre of evangelical leaders to write what became known as "A Declaration of

Evangelical Social Concern." The next year Ron assembled the same leaders and some others to discuss how this declaration might be enacted. I had the privilege of attending the second meeting. From there, the organization called Evangelicals for Social Action (ESA) was formed. My own thinking and response to Scripture have been shaped by interaction and friendship with the family. This organization has never had a large membership or a large budget but has continually acted as yeast in the body of Christ, producing results on a larger scale than any of us had ever dreamed. After becoming involved with ESA, I volunteered for various committees and task forces connected with social justice issues. I never intended to found an organization. I wanted only to take part in things that were already happening. As an ordained minister, wife of a pastor, career woman, and mother of four, I already had plenty to do.

Yet as I traveled throughout the developing world on various projects, I began to see a need that was not being met by existing missions or relief and development organizations. I saw the need for a way to empower people economically and educationally at a grassroots level. Beyond direct aid (sending food and money) I dreamed of providing education and economic development that would enable people to improve their own communities.

The director of world missions for my denomination, Dr. Don Bray, saw the need also. He and I began to study the issue along with Dr. Daniel Busby, now with Evangelical Council for Financial Accountability, and determined that a new organization was needed to meet the current needs in the developing world. I agreed to study the possibility, and after three years of examining the issues, we began a pilot project in Haiti that had the right focus.

I met in Haiti with a couple from the United States who was interested in investing their resources in the people of Haiti. We viewed the schools and listened to the hopes of the children. Finally, we asked, "What would you like for your school?" I expected them to list items like fans or soccer balls. To our surprise, they wanted computers. The next morning, we asked the local missionary what it would take to start a computer school. He was floored by the question. No one had ever thought of teaching computing there before. But before long, plans were under way to begin a computer school in the city of Petit Goave. Another goal was to begin a nursing school on the Island of La Gonave, where a single eighty-bed hospital serves the needs of one hundred thousand people.

In the end, funding was provided for both schools and an ice plant as well. Some thirty small businesses have been spawned from the ice plant, which also employs five Haitians full time. After that success it seemed that God was ready to start something new, but was I?

DECISION

After the Haiti experience, I knew that a decision had to be made. I needed to decide if I would follow this vision and take the leap or let the moment pass by. It was December 1995, and as I read the Christmas story one cloudy morning, the words of Gabriel seemed to jump off the page at me. The angel had come to announce to Mary that she would bear a child. Mary questioned the news, and Gabriel replied with these powerful words, "Nothing will be impossible with God (Luke 1:37). Overwhelmed and, I think, at peace, Mary responded, "Here am I, the servant of the Lord; let it be with me according to your word"(Luke 1:38).

I had quoted those words of Mary to others many times. Would I now be willing to risk my security on them? Did I believe that nothing is impossible with God? It wouldn't be easy to make that choice. I would have to resign my position as clinical director of a four-county mental health system. We had two kids in college at that time, and a third had just graduated, so we were facing several years of paying college bills. I had a vision for a ministry but absolutely no funds to go with it. That meant I would have no salary for the time being. In spite of all that, I felt convinced that starting this ministry was the right thing to do.

I phoned my husband, Wayne, at his office, and there seemed to be an extraordinary presence during our call. Wayne agreed that we should take the leap. I drove to my office and handed in my resignation, effective December 31. Almost immediately, a myriad of questions flooded my mind, questions for which I had no answer except this: nothing will be impossible with God.

FRUITION

In January 1996, I set up the first office of World Hope International in a bedroom of our parsonage in Warrenton, Missouri. I had a computer, a long table, and not much else. A friend began to volunteer her time to create promotional materials. She made a simple letterhead and produced some stationery at the local office supply. I put together a budget for the first year and couldn't help thinking, *This is truly impossible.* We assembled a board of directors, applied and ultimately received IRS non-profit status 501(c)(3).

On January 22 I had lunch with some friends to whom I had mentioned my dream in an earlier conversation. As we sat in the restaurant, I began to tell them about the things that were already happening in Haiti. We all began to cry, thinking about how God was working in the lives of people there. Finally, my friend asked, "Do you have a budget?"

"Yes," I said enthusiastically, displaying the operational budget I'd created.

"How much of this money have you raised?" he wondered.

I've never been one to beat around the bush, so I told him plainly: "Not one cent."

He and his daughter looked at the budget, then at each other. Then they turned to me with tears in their eyes. "You have now," he said. "We will pick up the whole thing."

Nothing will be impossible with God.

173

Before long, I was able to hire an administrative assistant and someone to help with Hope for Children, the child sponsorship portion of World Hope International. Within the next year, we turned another bedroom into an office. Finally, our youngest son, who was a senior in college at the time, volunteered his bedroom for a third office space. I tried not to act too eager, but he wasn't out of the house for two hours before we had stripped the walls and started painting. The one remaining bedroom in the house was ours, and somehow I knew that Wayne would not be in favor of giving it up! We eventually rented space in the downtown area of Warrenton. What a luxury it seemed! Even though the floors were a bit uneven, we had the room we needed. Finally, in the summer of 2000, we moved to a suburb of Washington, D.C.

From that humble beginning, World Hope International has conducted projects and programs in more than thirty countries, improving the lives of nearly one million people. In the United States, World Hope coordinates mentoring programs for families and children at risk. In 1999 World Hope International of Canada became an independent agency, and World Hope International of Australia was independently formed in 2000.

World Hope currently operates the largest micro-enterprise development program in the country of Sierra Leone. Recently, I had the privilege of celebrating the end of the first year of this program by announcing the 100 percent payback of all loans. As I entered the stadium in the capital city of Freetown on that warm February day, I was greeted by the sound of thousands of voices lifted in song. Here were people who had suffered unimaginable loss in the recent civil war, now singing with hands raised, "When I think of the goodness of Jesus and all he has done for me. . . ." My heart leapt at those words, and I joined my voice with theirs. How glad I was for that December day in 1995 when I put my trust in our Lord and his promise that "nothing will be impossible with God."

THE CALL TO HOPE

In spite of the successes, there have been days when I have wondered what in the world I am doing. When I lie awake at night trying to think of ways to balance the budget, knowing that the decisions I will make may mean life or death for some families, I feel hopelessly inadequate. Moving halfway across the continent resulted in the loss of staff members who had helped the organization to grow, but God has provided new staff with the skills needed for this phase of the ministry. Often, the financial uncertainties, the budget demands, and the challenge of leading the organization sometimes seem more than I can take. Yet the fear and pain are always balanced by the joy of seeing hundreds of thousands of people receive dignity and hope because of the ministry of World Hope International. Time and again, I fall back on the promise: nothing will be impossible with God.

The fear of failure prevents many people from making their hope a reality. That fear is real; failure is always possible. But as my mother told me when I was ten years old, selling Christmas cards door-to-door, success is never final and failure never fatal. Remember that hope is always filled with joy. Halley's song applies not just to five-year-old girls. I, too, am a promise; I am a possibility. And so are you. Together, we can bring God's kingdom to earth. That is the blessing of hope.

To Think About

1. What dream has God placed within your soul?

2. What has kept you from pursuing that dream? The fear of failure? The disapproval of peers? Feelings of inadequacy? Something else?

3. List some ways you can become involved in building the kingdom of God right now.

APPENDIX ONE

RESOURCES

Bread for the World
50 F Street NW, Suite 500
Washington, DC 20001
Tel: 202.639.9400 (800.82.BREAD)
Fax: 202.639.9401
www.bread.org
A Christian grassroots public policy organization working to eradicate
hunger with resources to engage local congregations, even to the children.
World Hope is one of the sponsors of the Annual Hunger Report.

Department of State
Undersecretary for Global Affairs on Sexual Trafficking
2201 C Street NW
Washington, DC 20520
Phone: 202.647.4000
www.state.gov

Evangelical Environmental Network
Rev. Jim Ball
c/o Riverside Baptist Church
680 I Street SW
Washington, DC 20024
www.creationcare.org
Publishes a quarterly journal in addition to resources for churches
and schools.

Evangelicals for Social Action
10 Lancaster Avenue
Wynnewood, PA 19096-3495
www.esa-online.org
Resources as well as current research.

International Justice Mission
PO Box 58147
Washington, DC 20037-8147
Phone: 703.465.5495
Fax: 703.465.5499
www.ijm.org
Pursues justice for the oppressed using two broad approaches: casework in the legal and law enforcement professions, and education in training people of faith to translate their convictions into active engagement.

League of Prayer
1526 Kimberley Lane
Prattville, AL 36066
Phone: 334.361.8497
Organization making worldwide impact in ministries of prayer and action with the "least of these."

Network 9:35
www.network935.org
Resources for reaching communities and networking with other organizations. World Hope is one of the partners of this network.

The Salvation Army
Initiatives Against Sexual Trafficking
615 Slater Avenue
P.O. Box 269
Alexandria, VA 22313
www.TheSalvationArmyUSA.org

World Hope International, Inc.
8136 Old Keene Mill Road
PO Box 2815
Springfield, VA 22152
888.466.4673
www.worldhope.org

APPENDIX TWO

THE CHICAGO DELARATION
OF EVANGELICAL SOCIAL CONCERN

As evangelical Christians committed to the Lord Jesus Christ and the full authority of the Word of God, we affirm that God lays total claim upon the lives of his people. We cannot, therefore, separate our lives in Christ from the situation in which God has placed us in the United States and the world.

We confess that we have not acknowledged the complete claims of God on our lives.

We acknowledge that God requires love. But we have not demonstrated the love of God to those suffering social abuses.

We acknowledge that God requires justice. But we have not proclaimed or demonstrated his justice to an unjust American society. Although the Lord calls us to defend the social and economic rights of the poor and the oppressed, we have mostly remained silent. We deplore the historic involvement of the church in America with racism and the conspicuous responsibility of the evangelical community for perpetuating the personal attitudes and institutional structures that have divided the body of Christ along color lines. Further, we have failed to condemn the exploitation of racism at home and abroad by our economic system.

We affirm that God abounds in mercy and that he forgives all who repent and turn from their sins. So we call our fellow evangelical Christians to demonstrate repentance in a Christian discipleship that confronts the social and political injustice of our nation.

We must attack the materialism of our culture and the maldistribution of the nation's wealth and services. We recognize that as a nation we play a crucial role in the imbalance and injustice of international trade and development. Before God and a billion hungry neighbors we must rethink our values regarding our present standard of living and promote more just acquisition and distribution of the world's resources.

We acknowledge our Christian responsibilities of citizenship. Therefore, we must challenge the misplaced trust of the nation in economic and military might – a proud trust that promotes a national pathology of war and violence which victimizes our neighbors at home and abroad. We must resist the temptation to make the nation and its institutions objects of near-religious loyalty.

We acknowledge that we have encouraged men to prideful domination and women to irresponsible passivity. So we call both men and women to mutual submission and active discipleship.

We proclaim no new gospel, but the gospel of our Lord Jesus Christ, who, through the power of the Holy Spirit, frees people from sin so that they might praise God through works of righteousness.

By this declaration, we endorse no political ideology or party, but call our nation's leaders and people to that righteousness which exalts a nation.

We make this declaration in the biblical hope that Christ is coming to consummate the Kingdom and we accept his claim on our total discipleship till he comes.

November 25, 1973
Chicago, Illinois

ORIGINAL SIGNERS

John F. Alexander
Joseph Bayly
Ruth L. Bentley
William Bentley
Dale Brown
James C. Cross
Donald Dayton
Roger Dewey
James Dunn
Daniel Ebersole
Samuel Escobar
Warren C. Falcon
Frank Gaebelein
Sharon Gallaghger
Theodore E. Gannon
Art Gish
Vernon Grounds
Nancy Hardesty
Carl F. H. Henry
Paul Henry
Clarence Hilliard
Walden Howard
Rufus Jones
Robert Tad Lehe
William Leslie
C. T. McIntire
Wes Michaelson

David O. Moberg
Stephen Mott
Richard Mouw
David Nelson
F. Burton Nelson
William Pennell
John Perkins
William Petersen
Richard Pierard
Wyn Wright Potter
Ron Potter
Bernard Ramm
Paul Rees
Boyd Reese
Joe Roos
James Robert Ross
Eunice Schatz
Ronald J. Sider
Donna Simons
Lewis Smedes
Foy Valentine
Marlin Van Elderen
Jim Wallis
Robert Webber
Merold Westphal
John Howard Yoder

NOTES

Introduction: What Does It Mean to Be Blessed?

1. Cited by Andrew Purves in *the Search for Compassion* (Louisville, Ky.: John Knox Press, 1989), 38.
2. Andrew Purves, *The Search for Compassion,* (Louisville, Ky.: Westminster John Knox Press, 1989), 40.

Chapter 1: The Blessing of Presence

1. Eileen Egan and Kathleen Egan, O.S.B.; *Prayer Times with Mother Teresa*; New York: Doubleday, 1989), 116
2. Henri Nouwen, *Seeds of Hope*, Robert Durbeck, ed. (New York: Doubleday, 1989, 1997), 126.
3. Ibid.

Chapter 2: The Blessing of Power

1. Wm. Barclay, *Matthew,* rev. ed., vol. 1, (Philadelphia, Pa.: Westminster Press, 1975), 70.
2. Henri Nouwen, *In the Name of Jesus: Reflections on Christian Leadership* (New York: Crossroad Publishing Co., 1989), 59.
3. Ibid.
4. Cheryl Forbes, *The Religion of Power* (Grand Rapids, Mich.: Zondervan Publishing House, 1983), 64.
5. Desmond Tutu, *No Future Without Forgiveness* (New York: Doubleday, 1999), 282.

6. Forbes, *Religion of Power*, 148.
7. Annie Dillard, *Teaching a Stone to Talk* (New York: Harper Perennial, 1982), 52–53.

Chapter 3: The Blessing of Holiness
1. William C. Martin, *The Layman's Bible Encyclopedia* (Nashville, Tenn., The Southwestern Company, 1964), 99.
2. Clara T. Williams, "Satisfied."
3. Dag Hammarskjold, *Markings* (New York: Alfred A. Knopf Inc., 1964), 100.
4. Ibid., 122.
5. Henri Nouwen, *Seeds of Hope*, Robert Durbeck, ed. (New York: Doubleday, 1997), 112.

Chapter 4: The Blessing of Loss
1. Richard Foster, *Prayer,* (San Francisco, Calif.: HarperSanFrancisco, 1992), 52.
2. Søren Kierkegaard, *Purity of the Heart Is to Will One Thing* (New York: Harper Torchbooks, 1956).
3. Søren Kierkegaard, *the Journals of Kierkegaard,* Alexander Dru, ed. (New York: Harper and Brothers, 1959), 245.
4. Mildred Bangs Wynkoop, *Foundations of Wesleyan-Arminian Theology* (Kansas City, Mo.: Beacon Hill Press of Kansas City, 1967), 118.

Chapter 5: The Blessing of Purpose
1. Karen A. Norton, *Frank C. Laubach* (Syracuse, N.Y.: Laubach Literacy International, 1990), 11.
2. Frank C. Laubach, *Thirty Years with the Silent Billion: Adventuring in Literacy* (Old Tappan, N.J.: Flemming H. Revell Co., 1960), 26–28.
3. Frank Laubach, *Learning the Vocabulary of God: A Spiritual Diary* (Nashville, Tenn.: The Upper Room, 1956), 20.

4. Frederick Buechner, *Now and Then,* quoted by Philip Yancey, *Soul Survivor* (New York: Doubleday, 2001), 259.
5. Laubach, *Vocabulary,* 9.
6. *Compassion and the Care of Creation,* Papers/Responses Presented at the First National Association of Evangelicals Conference on Poverty and Environmental Stewardship, March 18–19, 1999, Malone College, Canton, Ohio, p. 11. For more information on Evangelicals and the Environment see www.creationcare.org or www.healthyfamiliesnow.org.
7. D. Elton Trueblood, *The Common Ventures of Life; Marriage, Birth, Work, Death* (New York: Harper and Row, 1965), 86.
8. Philippe Vernier, "Action," The *Choice is Always Ours,* Dorothy Phillips, ed. (New York: Richard Smith, 1951), 354–355.

Chapter 6: The Blessing of Suffering

1. William Barclay, *The Letters of James and Peter,* rev. ed. (Louisville, Ky.: Westminster John Knox Press, 1976), 147.
2. Ibid, 149.
3. Ibid, 150.
4. Joanne Turpin, *Women in Church History*, (Cincinnati, Ohio: St. Anthony Messenger Press, 1990), 13–20.
5. Cited by Jim Collins in *Good to Great,* (San Francisco: Harper Business, 2001), 85.
6. Ibid.
7. Ibid.
8. Viktor Frankl, *Man's Search for Meaning*, (New York: Simon and Schuster, 1959), 97.
9. Ibid, 96–97.
10. Ibid.
11. Elie Wiesel, *Night*, trans. Stella Rodway (Hammondsworth, England: Penguin Books, 1960), 76–77.

Chapter 7: The Blessing of Reconciliation

1. Lisa Cahill, *Love Your Enemies* (Minneapolis, Minn.: Fortress Press, 1994), 31.
2. Richard Foster, *Streams of Living Water* (San Francisco, Calif.: HarperSanFrancisco, 1998), 172.
3. Richard Lovelace, *Dynamics of Spiritual Life* (Downers Grove, Ill.: InterVarsity Press, 1979), 370.
4. Ibid.
5. Ibid.
6. Foster, *Streams,* 176.

Chapter 8: The Blessing of Possibility

1. Jürgen Moltmann, *Theology of Hope,* (Philadelphia, Pa.: Fortress Press, 1993), 16.
2. *USA Today,* 15 September 1999.
3. Ibid.
4. N . Monk, *Orphan Alert: International Perspectives on Children Left Behind by HIV/AIDS* (Aids Orphans Database, www.orphans.fxb.org).
5. Jürgen Moltmann, "Jesus and the Kingdom of God," *Asbury Theological Journal* 48, no. 1 (Spring 1993): 8
6. "Agriculture in the Global Economy," *Hunger 2003—13*th *Annual Report on the State of World Hunger* (Washington, D.C.: Bread for the World Institute, 2003), 8.
7. Ibid., 19.
8. Ibid., 2.
9. Moltman, *Theology of Hope,* 22.
10. Philip Jenkins, "In with the underrated," *The New York Times*, 28 December 2002, A15. For further discussion of these ideas, see Philip Jenkins, *The Next Christendom* (Oxford University Press, 2002).
11. Bryant L. Myers, *Walking with the Poor,* (Maryknoll, N.Y.: Orbis Books 1999), 53–54.
12. Ibid, 236.

13. "A Program to End Hunger, Tenth Annual Report on the State of World Hunger," (Silver Spring, Md.: Bread for the World Institute, 2000), 13.
14. *Trafficking in Persons: USAID's Response* (Washington, D.C.: United States Agency for International Development, 2002).
15. Ted Olsen, "The Positive Prophet," *Christianity Today* (21 January 2003): 39.